ABOLITION AND THE AFRICAN AMERICAN STORY

ABOLITION AND THE AFRICAN AMERICAN STORY

RACE TO THE TRUTH

Patricia Williams Dockery

CROWN BOOKS FOR YOUNG READERS
NEW YORK

Crown Books for Young Readers
An imprint of Random House Children's Books
A division of Penguin Random House LLC
1745 Broadway, New York, NY 10019
penguinrandomhouse.com
rhcbooks.com

Editor: Kelly Delaney
Cover Designer: Jade Rector
Interior Designer: Jen Valero
Production Editor: Patricia Callahan
Managing Editor: Tisha Paul
Production Manager: Tim Terhune

Library of Congress Cataloging-in-Publication Data

Names: Williams Dockery, Patricia, author.
Title: Abolition and the African American story / Patricia Williams Dockery.
Description: First edition. | New York: Crown Books for Young Readers, 2025. |
Series: Race to the truth | Includes bibliographical references. |
Audience: Ages 10 up Crown Books for Young Readers | Audience: Grades 7-9
Crown Books for Young Readers | Summary: "The story of the Civil War
and Reconstruction from the African American point of view"—
Provided by publisher.
Identifiers: LCCN 2024050271 (print) | LCCN 2024050272 (ebook) |
ISBN 9780593811368 (trade paperback) | ISBN 9780593811375 (lib. Bdg.) |
ISBN 9780593811382 (ebook)
Subjects: LCSH: Slavery—United States—History—Juvenile literature. |
Reconstruction (U.S. history, 1865-1877)—Juvenile literature. | African Americans—
Social conditions—19th century—Juvenile literature. |
United States—History—Civil War, 1861-1865—Causes—
Juvenile literature. | LCGFT: Literature.
Classification: LCC E459 .W49 2025 (print) | LCC E459 (ebook)

The text of this book is set in 12.5-point Adobe Garamond Pro.

Manufactured in the United States of America
1st Printing

The authorized representative in the EU for product safety and compliance is Penguin
Random House Ireland, Morrison Chambers, 32 Nassau Street, Dublin D02 YH68,
Ireland, https://eu-contact.penguin.ie.

This book is dedicated to the beautiful babies and children in my life. Olive Scerpella, Sevyn Ayn Calhoun, Dion Dreni, and Renzo Thompson—you are my hope for tomorrow!

Acknowledgments:
Thank you to my research assistants, who helped me find credible scholarly sources and teacher resources. I couldn't have done this without you, Osayende Lessane, Aniyah Ruth Lessane, and Amanda Leske.
Thank you to Septima Poinsette Clark. You gave us the blueprint for development of engaged citizens. In times like these, I find myself asking, "What would Septima do?"

CONTENTS

INTRODUCTION

Depending on where you live or happen to be in the United States right now, the book that you're holding might be a banned book. It's true. In 2022, five states—Florida, Texas, Utah, South Carolina, and Missouri—enacted book bans to keep American students from reading books that promote understanding of diversity, including some aspects of American history, such as slavery, the Civil War, and the civil rights movement. This means thousands of American teachers are not able to teach students the complete truth about our nation's past, including the subject of chattel slavery and its enduring legacy in

American society, culture, and politics. In *Slavery and the African American Story,* we examined American chattel slavery, which is the enslaving and owning of human beings and their offspring as property, able to be bought, sold, and forced to work without wages. Although the term "slave" was used throughout slavery and much of the twentieth century, we use the term "enslaved people" to recognize them as humans rather than human chattel, or property.

By 2023, 182 United States school districts and thirty-seven states had banned nearly one thousand book titles (874, to be exact) covering a range of topics including slavery and African American history, but also books that examine sexuality, gender identity and inequality, and the history and mistreatment of other underrepresented American people.

Yet these stories, and the story of abolition in America, are necessary for understanding who we are as a people and as a nation. Acknowledging and honoring the contributions and experiences of BIPOC (Black, Indigenous, and People of Color) is one way we can collectively work toward making society more inclusive and equitable.

To do that, we will investigate seventeenth-, eighteenth-, and nineteenth-century grassroots (meaning organized by ordinary citizens) and political anti-slavery and abolition efforts to free those enslaved people and end laws created to discriminate against African Americans. These courageous Americans included people of all races working to create a more just society for all people. Some were political leaders, but most were everyday men, women, and young people.

Their courage and commitment to justice and liberty for all were the catalysts for seismic political change in the United States, including the abolition of slavery and the Fourteenth and Fifteenth Amendments to the U.S. Constitution. But they're often left out of the history of our country.

Think of it this way: What if someone wrote a book about all the people who live on your block to document what life was like when you lived there, but left you and your family out of the story? Would readers have an accurate and complete picture of what life was like on your block? Or would they have only part of the story?

Well, that's what's happened with a great many books about America. For many years free and enslaved Africans and African Americans were erased from history books. Their colossal contributions to every facet of American society were ignored by historians and other writers who documented American history, culture, and society.

That's also the case with the abolition and

anti-slavery movements in America. Few Americans know that the fight against slavery began during colonial times. As slavery became a part of American society, many citizens vocalized their opposition to the enslavement of African people and their descendants.

Abolition work was a family affair, with parents and children alike working to end slavery. Abolitionist mothers taught their children to hate slavery. Anti-slavery fathers modeled activism in the public square as speakers and strategists. Children as young as eight years old got in on the abolition action.

For some two hundred years the United States has led in technological innovation, global influence as a symbol of democracy, and inspiration for freedom-seeking people around the world. People from all walks of life make America great, and the nation's continued progress is made possible by the ingenuity and diversity of all who call it home. But many American history courses, books, documentaries, and museums have neglected to include the contributions of underrepresented people like enslaved Africans and African Americans and their descendants. Until the late twentieth century their lived experiences and accomplishments, and the roles they played in American society and culture, were erased or overlooked by writers, and in some cases by teachers.

The same is true with the American abolition and anti-slavery movements.

PEOPLE, POLITICS, PROGRESS, AND PROTEST

Uncovering the truth of how anti-slavery activism and abolition efforts affected American society requires acknowledgment of the enslaved *people,* whose contributions have often gone unrecognized, and of the politicians and activists who fought against slavery as well as those who supported it. It also requires looking deeply at history to investigate how the *politics* around slavery shaped and in some ways continue to shape American laws and Black life, health, and overall well-being today.

American progress and the country's rise as a world superpower were made possible by slave labor. Enslaved Africans, indentured servants, and hirelings (free African Americans and other people of color who hired themselves out for paid work) built the earliest towns and cities and provided skilled labor on Southern plantations during the slavery and Reconstruction eras and up through the mid-twentieth century.

Technological and industrial advances led to American economic progress and to prosperity for individuals and the nation as a whole. However, some of those revolutionary inventions were directly linked to slavery. Some others that are still in use today were created by Black inventors like Benjamin Banneker, who was the first African American to publish an almanac, in 1792. To this day, farmers use almanacs to track weather patterns so they know when to plant their annual crops. Of course, farmers today have many tools (like the internet!) for cultivating healthy crop harvests, but you can still find almanacs at most nurseries when it's planting time.

Even before the founding of the country, colonists used protests to voice their opposition to the tyranny of Great Britain. American patriots, including enslaved and free Black men, rallied together in violent protests that ultimately led to the American Revolutionary War. Likewise, Americans on both sides of the slavery debate used protest as a means for expressing their views on the issue. And once slavery was over, Black and white people alike protested about issues of voting rights, lynchings of Black people throughout the South, Jim Crow laws, police brutality, and civil rights.

By investigating American people, politics, progress, and protests during the seventeenth, eighteenth, and nineteenth centuries, we will gain a better understanding of how the nation grappled with American chattel slavery, the people and institutions that opposed it, the events and laws that led to its abolition, and how African Americans were affected by it all.

SANKOFA (LOOKING BACK TO MOVE FORWARD)

Sankofa is a spiritual and cultural symbol of the Akan people of Ghana, West Africa, many of whom were kidnapped and sold into slavery. The Sankofa symbol is most commonly depicted as a large bird with its head turned backward as a metaphor for looking back at one's ancestral history for guidance and wisdom, and avoiding mistakes of the past.

In *Slavery and the African American Story,* we uncovered the role slavery played in building what would become the United States of America. With this book, we continue to look back at American history to examine how the institution of slavery subjugated Black people, divided the nation, and inspired politicians, religious leaders, and everyday men, women, and children to fight to end slavery and free those living in bondage. Understanding their stories can help us ensure injustices like chattel slavery never happen again.

While the first official record of the transport and sale of African people in the American colonies happened in Virginia in 1619, Black people from Europe and Africa had already been traveling forcibly and by their own will alongside early explorers to the shores of what we recognize today as the continental United States of America. While some may wrongfully suggest that slavery was beneficial to the estimated four hundred thousand captured African men, women, and children (roughly 3 percent of the overall transatlantic slave trade) who were brought and sold in Southern and mid-Atlantic seaports, it was the opposite. Captured and taken from their homelands, they were enslaved by foreign people in a foreign land thousands of miles from families, friends, and loved ones. Children were separated from parents, and husbands and wives were separated from their children and one another.

Chattel slavery was a powerful and lucrative tool for American progress, and colonists would embrace slave labor to amass wealth, power, and influence. For two and a half centuries, first the colonies and then the United States grew in economic stature while the white people who lived here used enslaved people to fuel their industries, build their homes and towns, grow their food and export crops, and maintain their standards of living. What began as isolated cases of slavery in Northern and Southern communities grew into institutionalized slavery and eventually became a political issue that needed to be addressed by law—first by the colonies and then later at the federal level in the United States Constitution.

Millions of enslaved Africans and African Americans who experienced unthinkable suffering, subjugation, and oftentimes separation from family and loved ones—right here in the United States—made incredible contributions to American society and culture. Today the influences that African Americans and their enslaved and free ancestors have had on language, food, art, dance, medicine, math, biology, physics, anthropology, economics, architecture, literature, and politics are everywhere. But it is possible to miss their contributions even when they are right in front of your eyes. That's because much of African American history, and that of American chattel slavery, has been ignored, erased, and sometimes rewritten, making it difficult to see and understand how slavery shaped the young United States as well as American race relations even today.

It might interest you to know that just as chattel slavery was a part of colonial America before the founding of the United States, there were people resisting it and advocating the end of slavery from the very beginning. These early anti-slavery activists viewed slavery as immoral and unfitting for a nation of people who had themselves experienced oppression.

Free and enslaved Blacks and some white people resisted chattel slavery as far back as the American colonial era, and resistance took different forms. Many enslaved Africans did what they could, like running away and fighting back against slave catchers, overseers, and plantation masters to escape a life in bondage, while free Blacks helped fugitives they encountered by hiding and feeding them through secret networks of people committed to the anti-slavery cause. In the later years of slavery, brave people from all walks of life were clandestine operators who made sure the Underground Railroad stayed on track even before it had a name, invisible to crafty slave trackers and resolute slaver owners determined to find, retrieve, and punish their runaway slaves. The first white people to work to end slavery called on their religious leaders to take a stand against slavery to encourage fellow believers to take up the anti-slavery cause. Later, white anti-slavery advocates established organizations made up of people who believed putting an end to slavery was the best thing to do.

SOME COLONISTS OPPOSED SLAVERY

Even before the founding of the United States, there were colonists who were against slavery and actively working to end it. While abolition activism would not gain widespread traction and dedicated activists in the late 1700s and throughout the 1800s, formal opposition to slavery was first voiced a century before the founding of the United States of America. Roughly fifty years after the first twenty captured Africans were sold into slavery in Jamestown, Virginia, in 1619, four Pennsylvania Quakers drafted a petition calling for the end of slavery based on Christian doctrine.

Francis Daniel Pastorius and three of his fellow Quakers wrote the 1688 Germantown Petition Against Slavery, often simply called the Germantown Protest, arguing the need to end slavery because it was immoral and in conflict with the Christian "Golden rule" tenet, which instructs followers to treat others as they would want to be treated, and with the idea of the universal presence of God in all people and equality among all people. Pastorious and his co-conspirators saw themselves in those enslaved, suggesting their treatment was like the persecution Quaker societies had experienced in Europe as religious outliers, meaning they practiced Christianity differently from most other denominations. They used their common suffering to appeal to their fellow Quakers and other Christians to see the sin in slavery.

Unfortunately, the group's passionate decree didn't change the hearts and minds of colonial Pennsylvania slave owners, many of whom were in fact Quakers. Still, some followers would go on to be leaders in the anti-slavery and abolitionist movements of the next two centuries. Eventually, leaders of the Religious Society of Friends (the formal name of the Quakers) denounced slavery and forbade followers to own slaves in 1774. Quakers were the first colonial Christian denomination to do so. They were way ahead of their time.

By 1775, anti-slavery efforts were well underway by individuals who abhorred the subjugation and bondage enslaved Africans experienced. As the Founding Fathers worked tirelessly to free themselves and their fellow American colonists from the tyranny of the British monarchy, the Society for the Relief of Free Negroes, Unlawfully Held in Bondage, was established on April 14, 1775, in Philadelphia, Pennsylvania, to support abolition. Its name was changed in 1784 to the Pennsylvania Society for Promoting the Abolition of Slavery and the Relief of Free Negroes, Unlawfully Held in Bondage.

The society was founded by a Quaker schoolteacher named Anthony Benezet who was committed to doing all he could to help end slavery and educate Black children. Benezet was truly a forward thinker. At a time when the colonists were envisioning a new country where they could exercise freedom and the pursuit of happiness, Benezet was working for the freedom of the enslaved. But not only that; he taught enslaved children in his home and even opened the first school for girls in Philadelphia, at a time when white women were excluded from opportunities to learn and to organize. Benezet used his teaching skills to work tirelessly for gender and racial equity nearly two centuries before the women's and civil rights movements of the twentieth century.

Today we'd call Anthony Benezet a feminist, a Black Lives Matter ally, and a social justice advocate.

Like most American colonists, who fled oppression and limited economic opportunities in Britain, Benezet's family fled France, where he was born, due to religious persecution. The Benezets were French Huguenots, or Protestant Christians, who fled France at a time when non-Catholics were persecuted for their interpretation of Christianity and style of worship. Benezet knew a thing or two about oppression, and that fueled his anti-slavery activism. He was relentless in his desire to see slavery end, and eventually some members of the Society for the Relief of Free Negroes, Unlawfully Held in Bondage, convinced Pennsylvania state leaders to establish "gradual abolition" of slavery. Pennsylvania's 1780 Act for the Gradual Abolition of

Slavery freed enslaved people born in the state when they turned twenty-eight years old. Although it did not free all enslaved people in Pennsylvania immediately, it was the first act of abolition by any state.

When Anthony Benezet died in 1784, Benjamin Franklin became president of the Pennsylvania Society for Promoting the Abolition of Slavery and the Relief of Free Negroes, Unlawfully Held in Bondage. Franklin was many things, including one of the Founding Fathers who signed the Declaration of Independence and the United States Constitution. He also championed important causes like higher education and hospitals for the poor and mentally ill patients. Benjamin Franklin was also an anti-slavery activist.

However, like many whites of his time, Franklin held his own prejudice against Black people and, for a while, believed they were an inferior race. Franklin eventually had a change of heart—perhaps influenced by his friendship with Benezet and other anti-slavery supporters—and began to see Black people as equal to whites. With that shift in his thinking, Franklin took up the mantle of freedom for the enslaved.

As early as 1790, Quakers and the Pennsylvania abolition society boldly called on Congress to end slavery. And while Congress did not embrace their formal petition, Quakers were not deterred in their advocacy for abolition.

Throughout American slavery, Quakers led the way in establishing anti-slavery societies. In 1827 there were over a hundred anti-slavery societies throughout the South and another twenty-four in the North, with nearly seven thousand members altogether. By 1836 the number of anti-slavery societies had grown to over five hundred. Just two years later, that number had more than doubled and membership had grown to more than 100,000 anti-slavery advocates throughout the nation.

These organizations used overt (or visible) and covert (hidden, secret) tactics in the abolition cause. An example of overt anti-slavery activism is that by 1839, anti-slavery societies had gathered 2 million signatures on a petition calling on members of Congress to end slavery. Covert activism included members of anti-slavery societies secretly working as part of the Underground Railroad by hiding, transporting, feeding, and clothing fugitive runaways.

Throughout their existence, anti-slavery societies actively worked to disrupt American slavery. Their multiracial network of brave men and women used their voices and direct action through protests, to agitate slavery proponents and end chattel slavery.

"ANTI-SLAVERY" VS. "ABOLITION"

The meanings of *anti-slavery* and *abolition* are virtually the same. *Anti* means "opposed to; against something," and *abolition* means "the action or act of abolishing a system, practice, or intuition." However, during slavery, depending who you were talking to, they didn't necessarily imply exactly the same sentiment.

You may be thinking, "Well, if someone was anti-slavery, surely they wanted to *abolish* slavery!" And some anti-slavery supporters were also abolitionists, but not all of them believed freeing enslaved people was necessary. Some white people who supported anti-slavery efforts were more interested in stopping the spread of slavery throughout the country, rather than freeing the enslaved. They wanted the institution of slavery halted, often for political reasons, but didn't necessarily equate that with liberating the people who were enslaved.

For other anti-slavery supporters, ridding the country of slavery meant limiting slavery to the current slave states, or sending all the enslaved people "back" to Africa, even though by that time, most of the enslaved Black population had been born in America and had never been to Africa. We'll learn more about this movement in later chapters. They weren't at all interested in freedom for the enslaved. It's true; they only saw slavery as an unseemly and immoral practice that left a blight on America, and they gave little to no consideration to the lives of the enslaved.

Of course, there were many white people who were both anti-slavery advocates and abolitionists, which meant they wanted freedom for enslaved Africans and their descendants and the end of institutional chattel slavery in America.

As slavery spread throughout the South and made white Southerners richer and more politically influential, some Northern whites embraced abolition as a legal way to level the economic and political playing fields between the North and the South. Freedom for the enslaved would put an end to the prosperity and political power of the Southern planter class.

The point is that although there was opposition to slavery beginning in America's early years, those who opposed it very often didn't agree on what success would look like. By the 1800s, the abolition movement was widespread and championed by the Quakers, and free Blacks and whites of other Christian faiths were working for the complete abolition of slavery and freedom of all in bondage.

And by the time of the Civil War, abolitionists and Union soldiers and leaders—the men, boys, and even some women serving in the Union Army to defend and maintain the collective union of the United States—were fighting for the same cause: the end of slavery and freedom for the enslaved.

We will get to that in later chapters. First let's briefly examine some early United States history to uncover important contributions African Americans made to the nation that have been all but lost to the history books.

Our journey back in time begins in Washington, D.C.: the nation's capital.

CHAPTER I

THE COURAGEOUS CONTRIBUTIONS OF ENSLAVED PEOPLE IN AMERICA

Did you know the nation's most famous building was built using slave labor? That's right. Each year an estimated 1.25 million people visit the White House, where the president of the United States conducts business and lives with the First Family. It is a symbol of pride and hope for people from all walks of life. Yet many Americans don't know that it was almost entirely built by enslaved people. The origin stories of the White House and the U.S. Capitol Building are examples of how the contributions of enslaved Africans and African Americans are hidden in plain sight.

President George Washington had the dream of

building the White House, or the "President's House," as it was then called. In 1791 President Washington located what he believed was the perfect spot for such an important edifice. He enlisted the architect James Hoban to design it.

The White House was almost fully erected by 1800, due in large part to the construction work of enslaved people. The United States government didn't actually own the enslaved people who constructed the nation's most iconic building, although George Washington was a slave owner himself.

Instead, District of Columbia city officials "leased" them from their owners. Think of it this way: Enslaved African American were hired out by their owners, who earned income, like monthly rent on an apartment, for all the labor of masonry, painting, carpentry, and brickwork. The United States got a beautiful presidential manor, slave owners were paid for the work to build it, and the enslaved people who actually did the work got nothing.

Constructing a massive structure like the White House was not an easy feat! Enslaved people did all the arduous and backbreaking tasks, including log chopping, hand chiseling, and hauling heavy stones from nearby quarries. And they weren't riding in the massive cement trucks you may have seen at construction sites in your city or town. The quarriers transported stones and other material by oxen to a river, loaded it onto small sailing ships or schooners, and then sent it onward to the D.C. wharf, where it was unloaded and hauled to the construction sites.

City commissioners who were responsible for the construction of the President's House and the U.S. Capitol Building recognized that erecting such impressive monuments and the surrounding city would require a variety of talented tradesmen, and a lot of them. They first looked to Europe, hoping to find white men who were looking for an opportunity to come to America to do the work. When they failed to secure enough European laborers for the projects, they did what the original colonists had done: They got enslaved people to do the job.

We don't know much about the men who helped construct two of the nation's most revered historical monuments. We do know some of their names, the jobs they did, and the fees the slave owners were paid for their labor.

Construction of the Capitol Building was done by free men of color for meager wages, and by enslaved Black men, who received very little pay (if they were lucky) or no pay at all. Slave owners earned roughly five dollars per day for slave labor, and in some instances

A voucher for payment to slave owner James Clagett for work conducted by "Negro George." The receipt documents the length of work lease as five months and three days at "the President's House."

an enslaved person might receive a few pennies from a generous owner. In today's economy, that five dollars earned from slave labor would be worth about $170, while the three cents an enslaved person might be paid for his work would be a little over one dollar today. Some free men of color earned around a dollar a day, roughly $34 in today's economy. Both free and enslaved men could earn and keep any extra wages they earned working Saturday nights and Sundays. Even still, white slave owners took home the lion's share of wages paid for construction work on the U.S. Capitol.

Enslaved laborers most likely worked twelve-hour days—plantation hours they were accustomed to in grueling heat and humidity in summers, frigid temperatures in the winters. They had only basic tools, like pit saws—two-man saws—for cutting timber and clearing land and simple pulleys for lifting large stones and other materials.

President John Adams and First Lady Abigail Adams were the first presidential family to live in the White House. It would be over two hundred years, and forty-three presidents, before the first Black president and his family lived in the White House. President Barack Obama, First Lady Michelle Obama, and their daughters, Sasha and Malia, made American history when they became the first Black First Family and moved into a house that had been built centuries earlier by enslaved people.

• • •

The Statue of Freedom

Look closely at the top of the U.S. Capitol Building and you will see a bronze sculpture of a woman with a brooch inscribed with "U.S." In her hands she is holding a wreath of laurels, symbolizing American victory, and the U.S. battle shield with thirteen stripes

A diagram showing the Statue of Freedom atop the U.S. Capitol rotunda.

to represent the thirteen colonies. She signifies America's enduring commitment to liberty and justice for all people.

The irony is that it was the tedious and meticulous metalcasting work of an enslaved man that made her iconic image possible.

A plaster model of the statue was created and sent from Rome. But when it arrived in 1859, no one knew how to disassemble the massive figure so that it could be transported to a nearby workshop, where it would be cast, or molded, in bronze metal.

An Italian artisan had been brought in to do the work, but he quit abruptly over low wages. Clark Mills was the foundry owner who had been hired to cast the statue in bronze. But Mills couldn't do the job if he couldn't get all the pieces carefully taken apart and transported to the foundry.

Luckily, Philip Reid was there to save the day. Reid was an enslaved man owned by Mills who figured out a way to disassemble and transport the five sections of the plaster model to the foundry using a pulley-and-tackle system. At the foundry they reassembled the parts before casting the model in bronze.

THE REINS OF SLAVERY TIGHTEN

During the early years of the international slave market, whites purchased African people from West and West Central Africa who had been captured by European traffickers and, in some instances, leaders from other African nations. Over time, however, and especially after the United States passed the Act to Prohibit the Importation of Slaves of 1807, Black people born in America outnumbered those captured and brought to American shores. It was still legal to buy and sell enslaved Black people, just not those who were imported from Africa.

After this act was passed, foreign slave traffickers risked imprisonment for up to ten years, loss of their cargo ship, and a steep financial penalty—$10,000, or the equivalent of nearly $700,000 today—for buying or selling newly imported African people for use as slaves. Likewise, foreign shipbuilders, buyers, hired crew, and anyone involved with furnishing slave ships with food and other supplies faced imprisonment and a hefty fine for violation of the prohibition. Americans caught buying illegally transported Africans for use as slaves faced five to ten years in prison and fines from $1,000 to $10,000 for breaking the new law.

But the threat of imprisonment, loss of property, and expensive fines didn't deter international slave trafficking completely. In fact, some slave traders managed to maintain a lucrative business of importing slaves from Africa for fifty years after the 1807 act went into effect in 1808!

On September 16, 1858, a ship called *The Wanderer* arrived in the Congo (today the country of Angola) on a mission to illegally secure and secretly transport African people to the United States. It didn't start out as a slave ship. The previous year, Colonel John D. Johnson, a wealthy white Southerner from Louisiana, had paid shipbuilders to design and construct an opulent yacht to suit his personal taste and comfort. Upon completion, the *Wanderer* was a 238-ton, one-of-a-kind sailing vessel noted for its luxuriousness and ability to go up to twenty knots per hour. Yet the allure of his design didn't last long, and Colonel Johnson sold the luxury liner to William C. Corrie, a South Carolina man who believed the acquisition would gain him acceptance by the rich and elite communities of New York.

Little did Corrie know at the time that his purchase would take him in another direction entirely. Instead of currying favor among wealthy New Yorkers, Corrie went into partnership with Charles A. L. Lamar, a businessman from Savannah, Georgia. Although importation of slaves had been prohibited for fifty years, Lamar believed the federal government didn't have legal jurisdiction in state affairs, so he ignored the law. He convinced Corrie to accept a business proposition to travel to Africa and illegally purchase, transport, and sell captured Africans to willing buyers in the United States.

With a new enterprise before him, Corrie commissioned shipbuilders to remodel his luxury yacht so that it could clandestinely transport hundreds of captive men, women, and children in the bowels of the ship. Work being done to refashion the luxury schooner into a slave ship seemed curious to locals who observed the reconstruction. For example, one of the more dubious modifications was storage space for fifteen thousand gallons of water. Although many people speculated that these unique specifications were needed to conceal the presence of smuggled enslaved people aboard the vessel, Corrie's *Wanderer* passed all ship inspections, which meant Corrie and Lamar had the okay to set sail.

After avoiding the attention of the West Africa Squadron, a special British Royal Navy unit tasked with preventing African slave trading, the *Wanderer* arrived on the Congo shores. Once there, Corrie and Lamar enlisted the assistance of Captain William Snelgrave, an emissary of a thriving illegal slave-trading business based in New York.

Through Snelgrave's connections the men purchased nearly five hundred Africans, paying for them with rum, gunpowder, and weapons. After just under a month of negotiations, the men had concluded their transaction and were headed home with a cargo of captive people they were illegally transporting to sell in America.

Upon their return, the men felt victorious in their ability to skirt the law. Of the 487 captive Africans they had purchased, 78 had died at sea, leaving Corrie and Lamar with 409. They sold the remaining Africans in illegal slave markets in Georgia, South Carolina, and Florida. Although the men had been successful in getting the Africans to America, their activities hadn't gone unnoticed by locals, who alerted authorities about captive Africans being transported throughout the area. The men and their co-conspirators were investigated on suspicion of illegal slave trafficking, and the evidence revealed that they had falsified the ship's manifest documents. They were tried on three federal counts of piracy, but the Savannah jury that heard their case found the evidence insufficient to convict them. In the end, Corrie, Lamar, and the men who helped them were free, while the Africans they had illegally smuggled into the United States and sold were forced to live in bondage.

THE UNDERGROUND RAILROAD AND THE DISMAL SWAMP

We know a great deal about the Underground Railroad, a clandestine system of specific geographical routes, safe passages, and hiding places "conducted" by courageous Black and white people alike who risked their own safety to help enslaved people head north to secure their freedom. But not all runaways made their way north. Some found a safe and welcoming community much closer to the plantations they had escaped. Although they were just as important as northern destinations, less is known about these so-called Maroon communities, refuges for runaways in the Dismal Swamp, a vast expanse of wetlands in southeastern Virginia that once covered over 1 million acres of coastal geography.

The verdant area was a dense ecosystem of waterways, wildlife, trees, and thick brush inhabited by poisonous snakes, ferocious bears, and other wild animals—a dangerous place to hide from slave catchers and, given the dangers, not an ideal place to settle down and start a new life. British settlers who arrived in the early 1600s feared the inhospitable swampland was haunted. But for enslaved people forced to do agricultural work for seventeenth-century English colonists who had settled nearby, the dense and isolated wetlands hidden behind a canopy of ancient trees offered an option for escape.

They were welcomed by Indigenous people of Algonquian tribes who had been forced to settle there after violent encounters with colonists who took their land as their own. Living together, they became a Maroon society, a mix of people banded together, living in isolation from the white people who had been their captors and adversaries.

Over the years much of the swamp was drained, and many of its trees were cut down and sold as timber. Parts of it are now cities including Suffolk, Norfolk, and Chesapeake, Virginia.

Today what remains of the Dismal Swamp is roughly 112,000 acres of wildlife refuge that have been been preserved through federal conservation efforts. According to the U.S. Fish and Wildlife Service, the remaining acreage is a vestige of the once-expansive swamp.

OTHER MAROON SOCIETIES

During slavery, Maroon societies emerged as isolated, defiant, and self-sustaining communities living in some of the most impenetrable regions of the United States, South America, and the Caribbean. Beginning in the eighteenth century, free Blacks and formerly enslaved people from Georgia and South Carolina lived among the Seminole Indians in the Florida Everglades. Over time both groups adopted the other's customs and traditions and fought with them in battles against their sworn enemies: white men who wanted to capture, enslave, or remove them from the land they occupied.

John Horse, a Black Seminole leader, from an 1848 engraving.

American soldiers called the Florida Indians they encountered in the Everglades "Seminoles." The word *Seminole* comes from the Spanish word *cimarrón,* meaning "wild, untamed." They called the Black people living among them "Seminole Negroes." Today historians refer to them and their modern descendants living in Oklahoma, Texas, and the Bahamas as Black Seminoles.

HENRY "BOX" BROWN

Like the runaway enslaved people who risked their lives pursuing freedom in the miry morass of the Dismal Swamp, others took different but equally desperate measures trying to escape. Henry "Box" Brown was one of them. Brown, who had been born enslaved on a Virginia plantation in 1815, witnessed his entire family being sold off to other plantations. Later, as an adult with a wife and four children, Box suffered heartbreak once again when the members of his new family were all sold away to a plantation owner in North Carolina.

Both tragedies left Brown grief-stricken but more determined than ever to escape life in enslavement. He devised a clever but dangerous plan that required the help of two acquaintances who would pack him into a cargo crate and ship him from Richmond, Virginia, slave territory, to Philadelphia, where slavery had ended. Brown folded himself into the wooden box, which had three holes so he could breathe during the journey. Next, James C. A. Smith Jr., a white man Brown was friendly with, labeled the crate "Dry Goods" and shipped Brown off to the Pennsylvania Anti-Slavery Society. Upon delivery, Brown stepped out of the box, safe and sound, and recited a biblical passage from the book of Psalms, overjoyed about his safe passage to freedom.

The story of Brown's daring escape circulated widely among free Blacks and abolitionists, and he toured the region dramatically recounting his escape. As Brown's popularity grew among abolitionists, he created a panorama of painted scenes about his escape and the horrors of slavery. *Henry Box Brown's Mirror of Slavery*

Henry "Box" Brown emerging into freedom, from an 1872 drawing.

opened in Boston in 1850, just months before the passage of a new Fugitive Slave Act that granted slave catchers greater authority to search for and recapture escaped enslaved people in free territories. The new law made runaways like Brown vulnerable to capture.

Fearing the loss of his freedom, Brown stopped performing in front of audiences. Because of the risk of being captured and sent back into slavery, Brown left the United States for England, where he remarried and lived for twenty-five years before returning to the United States in 1875. He made a living as a performer and a magician, and one of his most awe-inspiring acts remained a lively recounting of how he had escaped slavery that ended with him popping out of the box that had delivered him to freedom.

LET'S THINK ABOUT THIS

1. Why is it important to recognize that enslaved Black men helped build some of our nation's most important monuments?

2. How did the 1807 prohibition of the importation and sale of Africans for slave labor both help and harm American anti-slavery and pro-slavery movements alike?

3. What are some strategies enslaved Africans used to escape slavery?

CHAPTER 2

TROUBLE BREWS IN THE UNION

The mid-1800s was a volatile time in America. The nation was deeply divided over the issue of slavery. On one side was the white planter class, which had become wealthy using generations of enslaved Black men, women, and children to cultivate its booming cotton, tobacco, rice, indigo, and sugarcane enterprises. On the other side were abolitionists who viewed slavery as inhumane and abhorred the subjugation and enslavement of Black people for profit. They were joined by some Northerners who wanted to end slavery not so much for moral reasons but to end the economic and political dominance of the South. Caught in the middle of the debate were roughly 4 million enslaved people whose lives hung in the balance.

As white men in the North and South argued, free and enslaved Black people took whatever measures they could to upend slavery, by either devising clandestine plans for escape or assisting other brave runaways in the journey to freedom. However, passage of the Fugitive Slave Act of 1850 made it nearly impossible for runaways like Henry "Box" Brown and others to maintain safe harbor even in free states—those where slavery was prohibited—because that new law required local and federal law-enforcement agents to arrest and return to captivity any known or suspected runaway slaves.

As early as 1643 American colonists were crafting and enacting statutes and laws regarding runaway slaves. In 1705 New York passed a resolution to prevent enslaved people from escaping to Canada. Others, including Virginia and Maryland, enacted legislation authorizing bounty payments for the capture and return of runaway slaves. Believe it or not, the United States Constitution included measures to prevent runaways from remaining free even if they made it successfully to a different state, including Article IV, Section 2, Clause 3:

*No Person held to Service or Labour in one State,
under the Laws thereof, escaping into another,
shall, in Consequence of any Law or Regulation
therein, be discharged from such Service or Labour, but shall be delivered up on Claim of the
Party to whom such Service or Labour may be
due.*

It may be hard to fathom that the same framers of the Constitution who had fought and won independence from Great Britain over its tyrannous treatment of the colonists, and who believed "that all men are created equal, that they are endowed by their Creator with certain unalienable Rights, that among these are Life, Liberty and the pursuit of Happiness" would deny the same rights to people living under the tyranny of slavery. But they did.

By the late 1780s and 1790s, there was growing outrage over slavery in Northern states, and many people pressured Congress to abolish it altogether. Southern pro-slavery supporters were equally committed to maintaining the "peculiar institution" of Southern slavery—a fictitious version of slavery where slaves benefited from their enslavement and were happy to serve their white masters. The newly formed Union was in trouble! With pressure mounting on both sides, the issue of slavery threatened the unity of the young United States of America.

Fearing the growing divide between Southern and Northern states over slavery, Congress passed the Fugitive Slave Act of 1793, which went much further than the fugitive slave clause written in the Constitution. It gave slave owners and their slave-catching agents authority to search for runaways in free states. If they caught a suspected runaway, these agents were mandated to bring the individual they had captured before a judge to prove ownership. In most cases proof of ownership was as little as a written statement or affidavit claiming the person held in custody belonged to the person who signed the document.

From the outset, Northerners actively pushed back on the Fugitive Slave Act of 1793, making it difficult to enforce. Some devised schemes to thwart efforts to recapture runaways by hiding those living among them or by creating safe houses as shelters.

Most Northern states established their own legislation to defy the Fugitive Slave Act of 1793, such as "personal liberty laws," which guaranteed a jury trial for captured runaways and legal protection for any free Blacks who had been ensnared by slave catchers eager to transport them to slave states. Many leaders and residents, wanting to thwart slave catchers who used violence and cunning schemes to kidnap unsus-pecting fugitive slaves and free Blacks caught in their crosshairs, used these measures to uphold their values.

Their methods were costly for white Southerners, who paid bounty hunters and lawyers a lot of money to secure the return of their "property." But slave owners were undeterred, and in 1842 the landmark Supreme Court case *Prigg v. Pennsylvania* would rule in their favor.

Edward Prigg was a slave catcher who had been hired by a Maryland woman named Margaret Ash-more to return Margaret Morgan, a "dower" slave—one whose ownership was passed down through inheritance—who had escaped. John Ashmore had granted Margaret Morgan many privileges, and her life resembled freedom in some ways, including being allowed to marry Jerry Morgan, a free Black man. Before his death, John Ashmore granted Margaret's freedom. But his heirs did not honor his wishes and argued he never fully emancipated her. That meant Margaret, and any children she had, were now the property of his heirs as part of their inheritance.

In a desperate attempt to live as free people, Margaret and Jerry fled to Pennsylvania, where per-sonal liberty laws provided cover and protection for freedom-seeking fugitive slaves. Despite Pennsylvania law, the Ashmore heirs were determined to get Margaret back. They enlisted an attorney named Edward Prigg to locate the young mother and bring her back to Maryland.

In 1837 Edward Prigg arrived in York County, Pennsylvania, to take Margaret into custody.

After securing a warrant from local authorities for her capture, Prigg kidnapped Margaret and her small children and transported them across state lines to Maryland.

It's probable that Prigg assumed that once he delivered the captives to the Ashmores, the matter would be finished. But he was indicted under a Pennsylvania act of 1826 that made kidnapping fugitive slaves and returning them to slavery illegal.

Prigg pleaded not guilty to the charges he faced, but in 1839 he was found guilty in the Pennsylvania court. When he appealed the conviction, his attorney argued that Prigg had acted in accordance with the fugitive slave clause of the United States Constitution, which gave slave owners the right to take custody of their escaped slaves wherever they were found. *Prigg v. Pennsylvania* made it all the way to the United States Supreme Court, which ruled that Pennsylvania's personal liberty act could not supersede federal law outlined in the fugitive slave clause. In their final ruling, the justices reaffirmed the supremacy of the fugitive slave clause and empowered slaveholders to use any means necessary to recapture enslaved people who managed to escape.

The *Prigg* ruling deepened divisions between Northern and Southern states. In the years ahead, chattel slavery would continue to be a major political issue that shaped state and federal laws and led to the bloodiest domestic military conflict ever fought on American soil: the Civil War.

Passages of the Compromise of 1850 and 1854's Kansas-Nebraska Act had far-reaching political implications for states' rights to self-govern and for the lives of millions of enslaved people in the antebellum South (the time period and Southern way of life before the Civil War). Together with federal judicial rulings like *Prigg v. Pennsylvania* and the *Dred Scott* decision, which you can learn more about in *Slavery and the African American Story,* both bills led to even greater dissension over slavery.

HENRY CLAY AND THE NOT-SO-GREAT COMPROMISE OF 1850

The United States experienced tremendous geographical expansion in the mid-nineteenth century. Through its military might, the young nation triumphed in conflicts with native Indigenous people and neighboring nations like Mexico. Each victory brought bountiful new territories, and with them new challenges to balancing political power between Northern and Southern states.

By 1850 leaders on both sides of the issue of slavery realized that arguing about it was never going to resolve the ongoing division over the matter. Something had to give. They needed a solution that appealed to both Southern and Northern states and wouldn't upset the balance of free states and slave states, giving one more congressional power than the other. But finding a solution proved difficult as leaders of Southern and Northern states dug their heels in over the newly acquired territories won in the Mexican-American War (1846–1848).

The Mexican-American War was a two-year battle over the location of the highly disputed Texas southern border and the U.S. president's wish to buy California and New Mexico. But it wasn't solely about "manifest destiny," the idea that America was destined to extend westward, acquiring more and more western territories along the way. Gaining Texas would be an opportunity to expand slavery even farther south!

When President James K. Polk's offer was rejected by Mexico's president, José Joaquín de Herrera, Polk got really mad. So mad that he sent troops to Mexico in January 1846 as an act of aggression, in hopes of inciting a war with the smaller neighboring nation.

Polk was so angry about not getting his way that he planned to appeal to Congress to declare war against Mexico. But Mexico beat him to it and attacked U.S. troops stationed near the Texas border at the Rio Grande. That was all President Polk needed to justify going to war with Mexico and ultimately defeating it.

For its victory, the United States gained approximately 525,000 square miles of Mexican territory, including California, New Mexico, and parts of present-day Nevada, Utah, Arizona, Colorado, and Texas. With so much new territory, U.S. politicians set out to ensure that the new states aligned with their views and the wishes of their state constituents on several interconnected issues: slavery, states' rights to self-govern with limited federal authority, economic and political factors, and cultural beliefs.

Slavery was at the center of all the issues. The addition of new states could upset the balance of free and slave states and thus affect the political and economic power of the North and the South. By limiting federal intrusion on state laws and practices, slave states could continue to permit slavery within their borders even if the federal government outlawed it.

Henry Clay was a Kentucky senator who worked to quell the growing division within the Union. Clay was an ambitious leader with an impressive career in state and national politics. In 1803, at the young age of twenty-six, he was elected to Kentucky's House of Representatives. Just three years later he was appointed to the United States Senate, even though by law he was too young to serve. Clay was twenty-nine, but the Constitution says senators must be at least thirty.

Senator Clay served in the Senate for sixteen years, was elected to the U.S. House of Representatives, and served as secretary of state under President John Quincy Adams. Early in his career he had made a name for himself spearheading the 1820 Missouri Compromise, which earned him the nicknames "Great Compromiser" and "Great Pacificator." While Clay never achieved his greatest ambition—to serve as president of the United States—his most tenuous and controversial political contribution, the Great Compromise of 1850, was a catalyst for the Civil War.

At the age of seventy-two and battling tuberculosis, an extremely contagious sickness of the lungs, Henry Clay used his diminishing strength to come up with a compromise that would prevent a civil war—a diplomatic strategy that would benefit Northern free states and Southern slave states equally. At the heart of the matter was the balance of existing and future free and slave states. Together with other politicians, the ailing Clay hotly debated all sides of the issue. At the end of six months Clay introduced the first federal omnibus bill, or legislative bill filled with many different acts, which he described as "neither southern nor northern. It is equal; it is fair; it is a compromise."

Much to Clay's disappointment, the omnibus bill failed. Political leaders on both sides of the issues didn't think it was a compromise at all. Southern states opposed any restrictions on slavery, and Northern states would not be forced to return escaped slaves living freely within their borders.

Yet all was not completely lost; Senator Stephen A. Douglas took Clay's failed omnibus bill and broke it into separate bills for congressional consideration. Douglas's five-foot-four height and gift of oration earned him the moniker "Little Giant." He used his political influence and excellent oratorical skills to revive support for the Great Compromise. He also used a different strategy to win the votes needed to turn Henry Clay's vision to law.

Instead of proposing one bill with several acts, Douglas introduced each act as its own bill:

- *California as a free state*
- *Abolition of the slave trade in Washington, D.C.*
- *The Fugitive Slave Act of 1850*
- *The possibility of slavery in future-established states within the western territories of Utah and New Mexico, which would be decided by their respective state governments*
- *Establishment of geographical boundaries of Texas*

When the congressional vote came up again, each of the bills passed and was made into federal law. The Little Giant had succeeded in doing what the Great Compromiser hadn't been able to: pass legislation to keep a volatile Union intact, at least for a little while longer.

But Northern and Southern Americans alike felt their side had not gotten what they wanted out of the legislation. Many Northerners who opposed slavery defied the Fugitive Slave Act of 1850; they could not and would not abide by the new laws. Though they passed, collectively, the bills increased brewing tensions between Southern states, which wanted to preserve slavery for cultural and economic reasons, and Northern states, which wanted to end slavery for political, economic, and philosophical reasons.

Protests, riots, and brawls regularly broke out between abolitionists and pro-slavery advocates, especially when slave catchers captured runaways in free states. That's because the Fugitive Slave Act of 1850 was much tougher than the 1793 law. Now local authorities were empowered to capture and return to their owners any people who escaped slavery, and anyone who aided their escape faced penalties, including harsh fines. More important, all citizens in free states were required to assist in the capture and return of any fugitive runaways living among them. Abolitionists doubled down on their efforts to help runaway slaves, with the Underground Railroad operating at full throttle. And some states, like Wisconsin, introduced bills to get around enforcing the Fugitive Slave Act altogether.

Thanks to Henry Clay and Stephen Douglas, and the passage of the Compromise of 1850, the United States temporarily avoided widespread domestic conflicts and the collapse of the Union—at the expense of enslaved people who escaped to gain freedom.

● ● ●

The Person Who Coined "Underground Railroad"

Between 1817 and 1861 an estimated hundred thousand runaway slaves made their way to freedom with the help of a social network of courageous people working throughout the Underground Railroad. The irony is that this secret transportation system was operating years before actual railroads became popular in the 1840s.

There are many theories about why it was given this name. Some have said it refers to the "disappearance" of escaped slaves on what was thought must be a railway that was literally under the ground. Others have said the term refers to the secrecy surrounding how it operated and the identities of the "conductors" who helped fugitives make their way to freedom. Until very recently the story of how this clandestine operation got its name was shrouded in mystery.

Thanks to one researcher's deep dive into the

archives of nineteenth-century newspapers, we now know Thomas Smallwood, once enslaved himself, gets the credit for naming the clandestine network. Scott Shane, a retired journalist, used his love of American history and newspapers to discover Smallwood and uncover why his story has remained a mystery for so many years.

When Thomas Smallwood bought his freedom in 1831, he could've simply lived his life in Washington, D.C., as a free man. But that wasn't enough for him. Instead, he thought it was important to help as many enslaved people as possible get to freedom. With the assistance of his friend and co-conspirator, a white man named Charles Torrey, Smallwood would load his wagon with up to twenty freedom seekers and help them escape to the North.

Slavery was legal in Washington, D.C., and although Smallwood was a free man, he was taking a big risk in trying to help people still in bondage flee. Smallwood's bravery didn't stop there. Using a pseudonym, he also wrote about his and Torrey's daring enterprise in satirical stories published in *The Tocsin of Liberty,* an Albany, New York, newspaper. Smallwood mocked white slave owners and brazenly recounted his and Torrey's success at delivering wagonloads of fugitive slaves out of slavery. Small-wood wrote about what sounded like an invisible train that magically transported runaway slaves to Canada, with himself as the train's conductor. If any-one had found out that he was the one writing those stories, Smallwood could've found himself back in shackles or even killed. But that didn't stop him.

Torrey later bought the newspaper and continued to publish Smallwood's stories, which began using the term "Underground Railroad" to describe the work of other abolitionists who helped fugitive slaves evade capture. Pretty soon Smallwood's image of an underground railroad caught on among other news-paper publishers, and writers in the North and the South began using it. Over time the term became a part of the American lexicon to describe the secret network of Black, white, rich, poor, old, and young freedom fighters who did what they could to help people escape enslavement.

Smallwood eventually had to make his way to Canada for his own safety. Although he stopped writing, his legacy lives on in every mention of the Underground Railroad.

SOLOMON NORTHUP

Solomon Northup wasn't always enslaved. In fact, he was born free in New York State in 1807. His father, Mintus, had been enslaved but was emancipated by his owner upon his death. Growing up, young Solomon helped his father till the land on the family farm. As a youngster, he also had some formal education, and by adulthood he could read and write. This was quite unusual for Black people at this time! Solomon was also a gifted musician—he was a popular fiddler who enjoyed entertaining local audiences.

In 1828, with a farm of his own, Solomon married Anne Hampton, and the two started their family. A few years later the couple decided to seek out other opportunities to support the family, which had grown to include three children. In 1834, they sold their farm and moved to Saratoga Springs, New York. Together they worked a variety of jobs to sustain their family, and Solomon's notoriety as an entertaining fiddler grew.

One day Solomon was approached by two men, James H. Burch and Ebenezer Radburn, who offered him the opportunity to work with them as a paid fiddler as they made their way back to their circus in Washington, D.C. If he agreed to accompany them and to play the fiddle for audiences between Saratoga Springs and New York, they would pay him one dollar for each performance—close to thirty-seven dollars in today's money—as well as the cost of returning home once he had fulfilled his obligation. Solomon jumped at the chance to support his family by playing the fiddle.

Little did he know that the two "recruiters" were actually slave dealers who made their living kidnapping fugitive freedom seekers and unsuspecting free Black people alike and selling them to slave owners in the deep South. They had woven an elaborate story to dupe the unsuspecting Solomon into willingly traveling with them.

Taking only his fiddle and a few other items, Solomon climbed into their wagon, unaware of the dastardly scheme they had planned. The devious crooks got him far from his home and then beat him repeatedly so that he would be afraid to tell anyone his true identity. After several days of traveling, Solomon found himself drugged and trapped, with no help in sight. He had been transported to Washington, D.C., where he was severely beaten again and then sold off to a Louisiana slave owner. He would spend the next twelve years enslaved, and his family had no idea what had happened to him.

Solomon, who had lived a happy and relatively simple life, now found himself living in a nightmare. And things only got worse when he was sold to a violent and barbaric plantation owner named Edwin Epps.

A chance meeting with abolitionist Samuel Bass changed his fate. When Bass delivered letters to Solomon's wife to alert her to his dreadful circumstances, she enlisted the help of white friends, who petitioned for his freedom. Luckily for him, there was a New York law that citizens who were unlawfully sold into slavery had to be returned. With the law on their side, Solomon's friends were able to rescue him and free him from the clutches of slavery once and for all.

THE KANSAS-NEBRASKA ACT

By 1854 Stephen Douglas had turned his political influence toward the undeveloped western frontier. He wanted to develop a transcontinental railroad from Chicago, in his home state of Illinois, to the vast Nebraska Territory (which included Kansas, Nebraska, Montana, and the Dakotas) as a way to transport people and expand American business enterprise.

And since land in the new territory was free and available for any settlers who wished to live in the unruly, wild West, abolitionists and slaveholders saw staking their claims there as the best way to promote their side of the slavery issue. In reality, of course, the Nebraska Territory was uncharted only by white people; Indigenous people had been inhabiting the region for tens of thousands of years.

Douglas's vision for the Nebraska Bill, as it was originally called, was one of expansion and innovation. There was a problem, however; one design for the railway route went through a region where slavery had been prohibited over thirty years before. Remember the 1850 Compromise that Henry Clay couldn't get Congress to approve? Douglas had adopted a different strategy that had parts of the bill voted on separately, instead of as one mega bill. Then he and his political allies worked to persuade other members of Congress to vote in favor of each of the five bills. In the end, Douglas succeeded where Henry Clay had failed; Congress enacted the five bills that made up Douglas's failed omnibus bill.

The Compromise of 1850 outlawed slavery in parts of the territory acquired in the 1803 Louisiana Purchase (when the United States paid a lot of money for 530 million acres of North American land from

France)—specifically, modern-day Kansas, Nebraska, Montana, and North and South Dakota, right where the transcontinental railroad would run. Louisiana had been a French colony way back in the late 1600s, when it was claimed by a French explorer named René-Robert Cavelier de La Salle. The territory was sold back and forth between France and Spain until France sold it to the United States.

Although the 1820 Missouri Compromise prevented expansion of slavery into western terrains in the Lousiana Purchase, Douglas was undeterred. He wanted forward progress for the nation, and he believed an expansive and advanced railroad to the newly acquired western territory would do the trick. But getting support proved more difficult than he anticipated.

Southern states and pro-slavery advocates wanted to permit slavery throughout the Louisiana Territory and have the transcontinental railway travel through the South, beginning in Texas, which had been admitted as a slave state. Northern states and abolitionists wanted assurance that the letter of the law, as outlined in the 1820 Missouri Compromise, would be followed. One of the major goals of the bill was to ensure balance between the numbers of free and slave states. That meant slavery would be prohibited in any new territory north of the Missouri Compromise boundary.

Douglas came up with a plan that would appease

both sides—or so he thought! Any new states established out of the Nebraska Territory would use "popular sovereignty"—a fancy way of saying a majority vote would decide if they would allow or prohibit slavery within their borders.

But Northern representatives were incensed that the proposed law could very well pave the way for an increasing number of slave states and thus spread the inhumane practice throughout the nation.

Southern leaders saw the bill as a barrier to expanding their prosperity and way of life because it did not explicitly allow slavery in the new region. They demanded the repeal of the Missouri Compromise outright!

Although he knew repealing the earlier law would upset the balance of free and slave states, Douglas included the repeal of the 1820 Missouri Compromise anyway. Douglas himself was a slavery proponent, and he was supporting the interests of like-minded political leaders and citizens. Douglas also wanted the railway really badly!

Once again Douglas tried to use his "gift of gab" and political influence to win consensus for his ideas. He spent many hours cajoling disgruntled senators, pleading with them to pass the bill. And they did. The measure passed 37–14 and became law May 30, 1854.

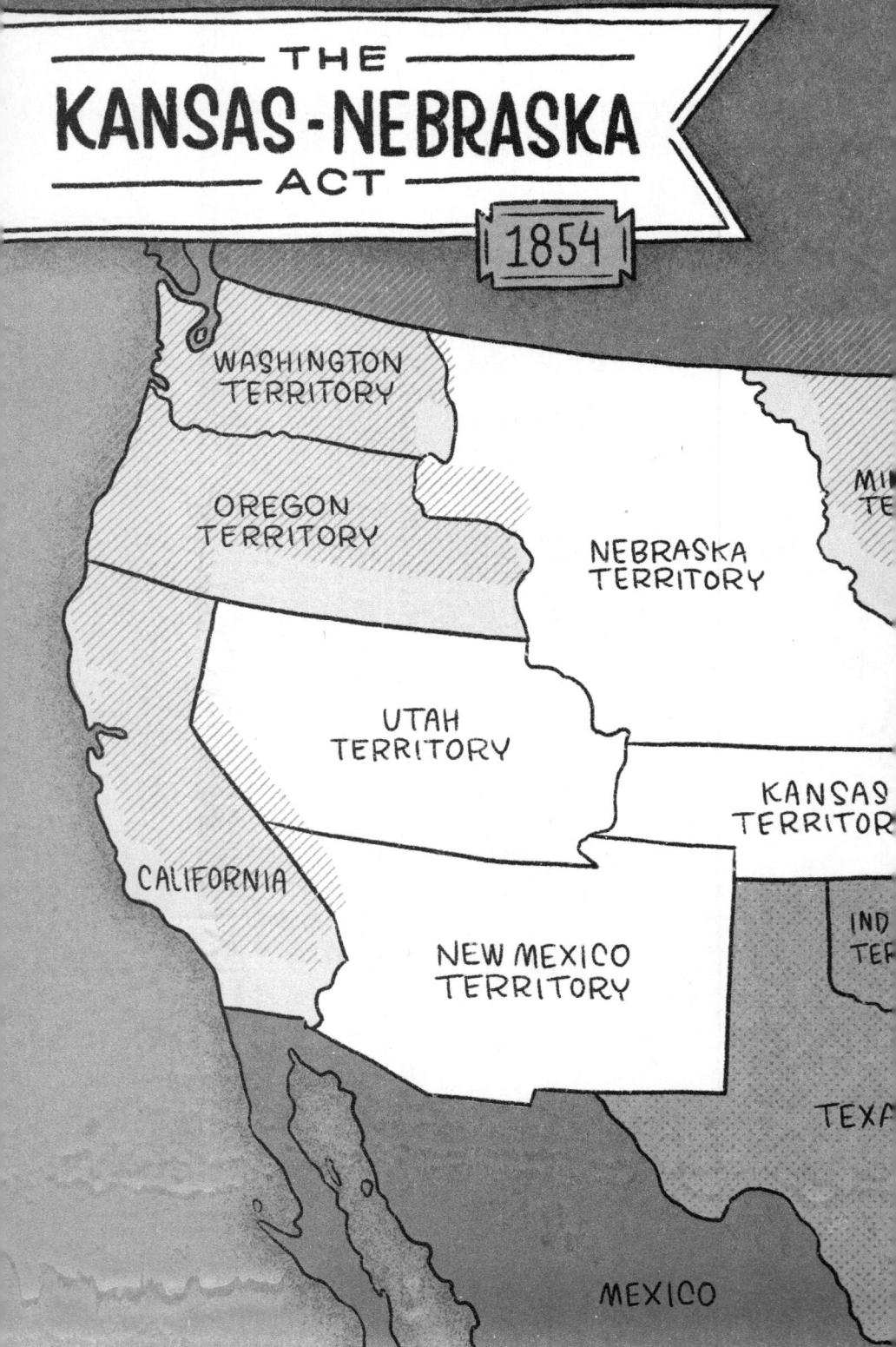

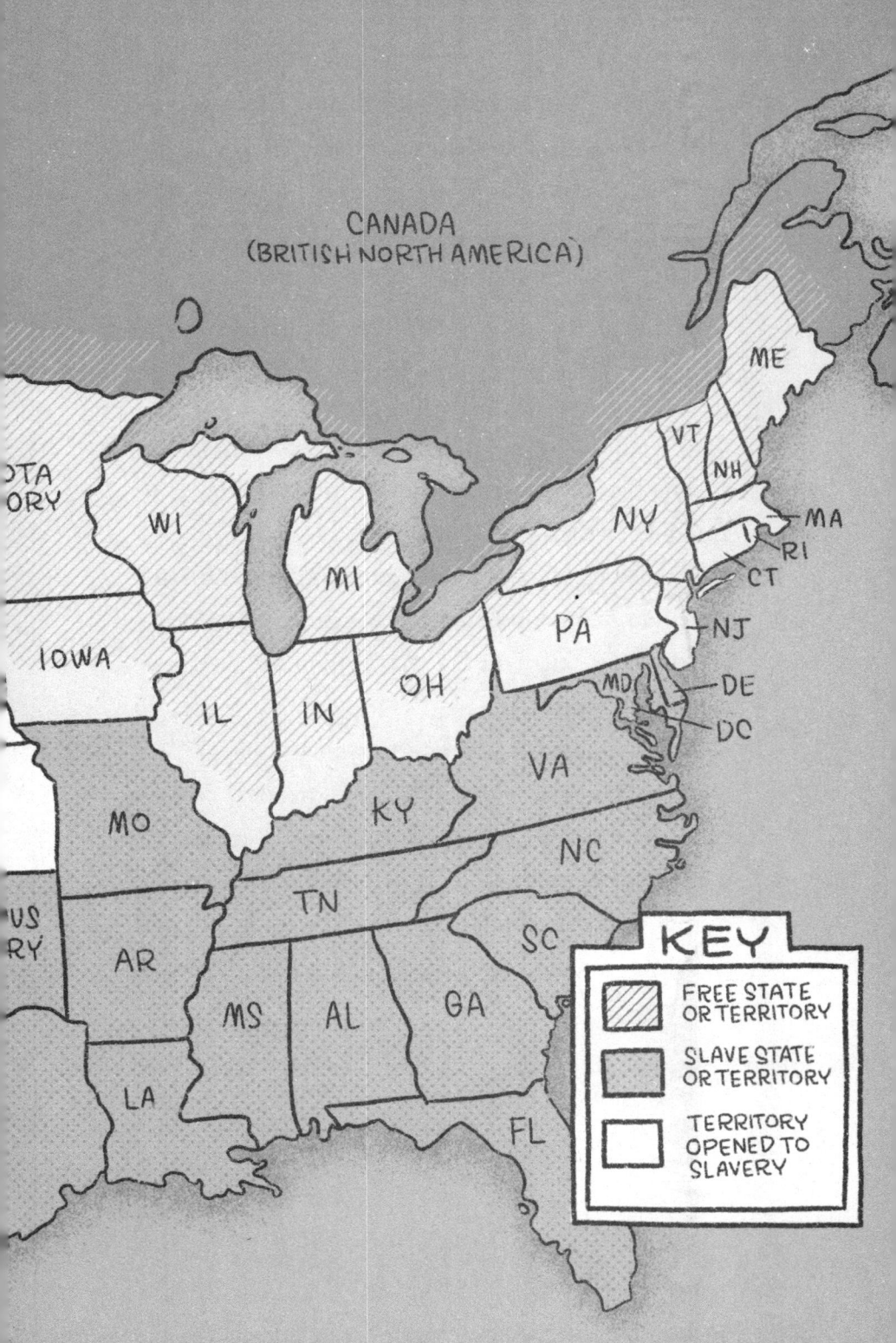

Stephen Douglas had done it again. This compromise was a personal victory; he believed the transcontinental railroad would usher in prosperity and continued progress for the country.

Little did he know that it would have the exact opposite effect. Passage of the Kansas-Nebraska Act was a political powder keg that left the United States on the verge of explosion. People, protests, and publications would stoke the embers and lead to widespread violence, domestic unrest, and ultimately the first and only civil war in United States history.

In the end the heated debate around the Kansas-Nebraska Act focused more on the issue of American chattel slavery than on Douglas's vision for his transcontinental railroad.

What Douglas had set in motion would split up his own political party—the Democratic Party—derail his political dream of becoming president of the United States, and pave the way for an up-and-coming anti-slavery politician from Illinois to win the presidency and end slavery once and for all.

JOHN BROWN

After the passage of Douglas's bill, countless everyday Americans and business speculators saw the Nebraska frontier as ripe with possibility, and they packed up their belongings and headed west to forge a new life. They weren't the only ones to heed the call of the untamed Western front: abolitionists and pro-slavery advocates made their own mad dashes to stake their claims on land they hoped would soon be part of new free or slave states added to the Union.

They would clash in violent conflicts known as "Bleeding Kansas." The vicious altercations ended with the deaths of many Americans, panicking terrified citizens and increasing tensions among politicians and activists alike.

In the following years several famous events, publications, and people would fan the political flames that would eventually engulf the country in the bloodiest conflict between American people on American soil the country has ever experienced: the Civil War. John Brown was one of them.

John Brown is probably the most controversial abolitionist to have lived. He was a fearless white activist willing to sacrifice his life for the cause. Born in 1800 in Torrington, Connecticut, to pious Christian parents who believed slavery was wrong, Brown worked as an abolitionist, influenced by his parents' anti-slavery sentiment. When he was a child, his parents moved the family to Hudson, Ohio, which was a stop on the Underground Railroad. There, his father, Owen Brown, became active in efforts to get runaway slaves to free states, and their home became a clandestine haven for passengers on the Underground Railroad. His parents also befriended Indigenous people who had lost their land to American expansionism.

Throughout his life John Brown suffered many heartbreaks. He lost his first wife and two of his children to illness, some of his businesses failed, and he filed for bankruptcy to cut his financial losses. In 1833 he remarried and started a new family.

With a new lease on life, Brown moved his family to Springfield, Massachusetts, to start over again. As soon as Brown and his family were settled, he began getting acquainted with the abolitionist community there. In 1850 Brown uprooted his family once again, this time moving to Timbuctoo, a farming community in New York State's Adirondack Mountains, at the invitation of abolitionist Gerrit Smith, who used his influence and wealth to help Blacks acquire land for farming in the area. Smith was a strategic abolitionist who put his money where his mouth was by helping free Blacks purchase land. Back then, only men could vote, and because land ownership was a prerequisite, Black people were mostly barred from voting. From Smith, Brown learned cunning ways to help Black people outwit the system.

In nearby Lake Placid, New York, Brown purchased land for farming. There, on his farm, Brown met with, advised, and supported the efforts of Black abolitionists in the area.

Brown wasn't just committed to exposing the violent and inhumane nature of slavery. He was a radical abolitionist who fully embraced violence as the most effective means to end slavery. Brown's belief that God had ordained him to do whatever was necessary to free enslaved Blacks was a far cry from the pacifist leanings of the Quakers' Religious Society of Friends, many of whom were also

A portrait of John Brown completed between 1846 and 1847.

conductors on the Underground Railroad by that point.

Like many abolitionists, Brown was disappointed and angry when the 1850 Fugitive Slave Act was passed. But when the Kansas-Nebraska Act was made law, Brown's fiery ire was ignited! The federal government's support for slavery galvanized Brown. Abolitionists and other anti-slavery citizens who had flooded the Nebraska Territory to stake their claims for a free state found themselves outnumbered and outgunned. When word of the abolitionists' troubles in the new territory reached Brown, he became so enraged that he gathered firearms and headed westward to assist the outnumbered abolitionists in the new territories.

BLEEDING KANSAS

In the spring of 1855, Brown's older sons moved to Kansas to fight against the spread of slavery. Brown and other family members settled near the Osawatomie River in Kansas in October of that year. Armed with rifles, pistols, and a thousand pikes (long wooden spears with metal blades at the tips) and flanked by his five sons, his son-in-law, and two other men,

Brown was determined to stamp out slavery by any means necessary. In 1856 the city of Lawrence, Kansas, was besieged by pro-slavery hooligans, and Brown learned that Massachusetts senator Charles Sumner, his anti-slavery ally, has been brutally physically assaulted in public in the United States Capitol Building in Washington, D.C., by a fanatical South Carolina representative, Preston Brooks. Brown's resolve as a fierce anti-slavery vigilante hardened.

John Brown's legacy was sealed by two very brazen and brutal attacks against the institution of slavery. First, on May 24, 1856, Brown led a contingent of five men on a killing spree that ended with the brutal murder of five pro-slavery men. Known as the Pottawatomie Massacre, this depraved assault in the name of abolition made Brown a feared radical in the cause that meant so much to him. Over the years he had become friends with Frederick Douglass and Harriet Tubman, but neither of these outspoken freedom fighters supported Brown's belief that slavery would be ended only by violence. Brown's violent means to end slavery were rejected by some of the very people he was fighting for!

Brown wasn't fazed by his friends' lack of support for his mission. He believed that he had been "called by God" to mete out violent punishment, if necessary, to end slavery. He enlisted the help of formerly enslaved people, his own sons, and other white allies to lash out against pro-slavery advocates and government officials, striking fear in the hearts and minds of white Southerners.

But the Pottawatomie Massacre was just the beginning for Brown. On October 16, 1859, Brown led a group of men on a bloody mission to capture a public official and seize the government armory at Harpers Ferry, West Virginia. The planned attack was symbolic and deliberate. First they kidnapped Colonel Lewis William Washington, who was a relative of President George Washington. When he learned of Colonel Washington's identity and that he lived in Harpers Ferry, Brown had set his sights on the Washingtons as targets in his raid. That's because the Washington family owned enslaved people, and Brown wanted the attack to symbolize the penalties for anyone who supported slavery.

Even more important, the brazen attack on the armory was a deliberate attempt to seize weapons and weaken governmental support for slavery. Brown and his men took several captives during the melee, but they were eventually outnumbered by a local militia that formed as a result of the raid.

By the time the raid was over, four residents,

including the mayor and one of Brown's sons, had been killed. During the attack Brown's men killed a free Black man they had detained after an encounter on a train en route to the nation's capital. The slain man was a baggage handler on the train who defied Brown's men.

Upon hearing about the attack and casualties, President James Buchanan enlisted Colonel Robert E. Lee to lead a company of ninety marines to Harpers Ferry to put an end to Brown's reign of terror.

At first Colonel Lee attempted to get Brown to surrender. But when that failed, Lee ordered his men to storm the fort where Brown and his men were holed up, rescuing the hostages and capturing the wily vigilante John Brown. For his crimes against the government, Brown was tried and convicted of treason and sentenced to execution. He was hanged on December 2, 1859.

While it is true that Brown's plan ultimately failed, what cannot be discounted is the impact his actions had on slave owners and pro-slavery advocates. Brown's zeal, courage, and resolve to end slavery by any means necessary terrified white people in the North and the South.

BLACK PEOPLE ALSO MADE THEIR WAY WEST

Here in the United States, people often discuss "how the west was won," referring to the settlers and pioneers who ventured out west and claimed territory. History books, television shows, and movies include depictions of rifle-toting cowboys who subdued lawless "Indians" on the western frontier. Rarely told is the story of Black Exodusters—freed Black people who left the South and made their way to places such as Oklahoma, Nebraska, Kansas, Ohio, North Dakota, South Dakota, Montana, New Mexico, and Arizona. In the 1870s alone, upward of 60,000 Southern Blacks heeded the call of the west. By the end of 1880, 41,000 Black Kansans had joined the state's population.

Benjamin "Pap" Singleton was a businessman and real estate investor who believed Black people could create better opportunities for themselves in Black Canaan, or the Promised Land, out west. He gave himself the nickname "Moses of the Colored Exodus" to portray himself like the biblical figure Moses, who led the Israelites out of Egypt into Canaan. When he settled in Kansas and established "Singleton's Colony," he brought three hundred Southern

Black Exodusters with him. He wasn't the first or the last Black pioneer to stake a claim on a new life in this area.

Many Black Exodusters chose Kansas because it was easier to get to from the South than other places farther west, it had plentiful land that was relatively cheap, and it had been made notorious by John Brown, who had fought for the freedom of Black people. Over time, Black settlers established towns, mixed with and married Indigenous people, and created a rich culture and traditions that still remain.

Have you ever watched a Western movie? The odds are you haven't. Westerns lost popularity with moviegoers over fifty years ago, but chances are your parents and grandparents are familiar with action-packed Western films that featured crafty renegade outlaws and upstanding lawmen dedicated to maintaining law and order. These popular films were set in harsh, violent frontier towns and Indigenous villages of the American West. Famous American actors like John Wayne, Glenn Ford, and Clint Eastwood portrayed cowboys, gunslingers, and upstanding and courageous lawmen, while Indigenous Americans were depicted as violent and wild primitive people who often found themselves on the wrong side of the law. When Black people appeared in these films, they usually played stereotypically subservient roles as servants such as maids and cooks. The writers and producers of these films used American cinema to promote white supremacist ideals through the characters and storylines.

William "Bill" Pickett was the first Black cowboy movie star. But Bill Pickett didn't just portray a cowboy on the big screen—he actually was one in real life. Pickett was a rodeo performer of African American and Indigenous ancestry. Born in Travis County, Texas, in 1870, he was famous for "bulldogging," or cattle wrestling, a popular attraction at rodeos throughout the United States. Pickett's unique and unconventional technique involved grabbing a steer by the horns, twisting its neck, and biting it on the nose or upper lip to force it down on its side. Pickett gained notoriety for his talent as a cattle

The movie poster for The Bull-Dogger, *starring Bill Pickett.*

wrestler, and eventually he and his brothers decided to start Pickett Brothers Bronco Busters and Rough Riders. The Pickett brothers specialized in "catching and taming wild cattle."

After beginning when he was just eighteen years old, in 1888, Bill Pickett had a long and successful career as a rodeo performer. For more than a quarter of a century Pickett performed as the "Dusky Demon."

Bill made a name for himself shortly after entering his first rodeo, winning countless competitions against white cowboys. However, since Black people were not allowed to compete with or even occupy public space with white people as equals, Pickett was able to enter the contests only by claiming he was Indigenous. In Texas it was acceptable for Indigenous riders to compete in rodeos, but not Black riders.

Bill Pickett's success didn't stop with the Texas rodeo; he went on to appear as a Black cowboy in several early-twentieth-century movies, including *Crimson Skull* (1921) and *The Bull-Dogger* (1922), making him the first Black actor in American Westerns. With fame, he no longer had to hide his race behind the "Dusky Demon" character.

BASS REEVES

While Bill Pickett's cinematic portrayal of Black cowboys has been etched into American film history for over a hundred years, Bass Reeves's legacy as a daring federal agent who single-handedly brought countless criminals to justice is just now making its debut in film, television, and some history classes.

Reeves is credited with being one of the most successful U.S. marshals west of the Mississippi River, having arrested over three thousand wanted criminals and killed fourteen of them. His life's journey from slave to American law-enforcement hero sounds like a story written for the big screen. In fact, historian Art Burton believes Reeves's success as a U.S. marshal inspired the creation of the Lone Ranger, a popular film, radio, and television character during the mid-twentieth century who was a masked ranger with an Indigenous sidekick who traveled the wild West bringing criminals to justice. According to Burton, the show and its characters share striking similarities to Bass Reeves's real-life story, except the Lone Ranger is portrayed as a masked white man, not a Black one. While there are historians who doubt Burton's claims about Reeves being the inspiration behind the fictitious television hero, he points out several similarities to support his theory. Reeves gave out silver dollars and the Lone Ranger gave out silver bullets; the Lone Ranger wore a black mask, which could represent a Black man's face; and, just as the series ended with characters asking, "Who was that masked man?" white people who encountered Reeves could only identify him as "the Black marshal."

Although Reeves was born enslaved in Crawford County, Arkansas, in 1838, as a free man he led a storied life of danger and adventure in which he legally put the shackles on thousands of white outlaws.

Reeves was owned by William Reeves, who in 1846 moved his family and slaves to Grayson County, Texas. Years later, during the Civil War, Reeves escaped slavery, fleeing to Indigenous territory—today we call it Oklahoma.

There, living among the Five Tribes (Cherokee, Chickasaw, Choctaw, Seminole, and Muskogee), Bass Reeves became a *polyglot*—someone who speaks multiple languages. But he not only learned the languages of the Five Tribes, he also learned their customs and skills, such as tracking, the ability to locate enemies using knowledge of the layout of the geographic territory.

Like many formerly enslaved people, Reeves couldn't read or write, but he did have an excellent memory. As a lawman, Reeves didn't read the arrest warrants for the criminals he caught. He'd recite what the judge had written in the warrant that gave him the authority to capture, arrest, and return fugitives living within his jurisdiction. To do this, he would have someone read the warrants over and over until he could memorize them word for word.

Bass Reeves was also a revered marksman. Unlike most shooters, he could shoot pistols and rifles using either his right or left hand. Standing six feet two inches and weighing nearly two hundred pounds, Reeves was an imposing figure who could fight two men at a time and win!

Reeves was a dogged marshal who went to great lengths to catch bandits, outlaws, and fugitives, including dressing in different disguises so no one would suspect he was a law-enforcement agent on the hunt for criminals with outstanding warrants for their arrest. Reeves was a supersleuth who transformed himself into many different characters to conduct effective detective work that resulted in countless arrests.

These unique talents appealed to U.S. marshal James Fagan, who needed to find and hire two hundred new deputy marshals to patrol and protect "Indian territory," the vast southwest lands inhabited by Indigenous people west of the Mississippi River, excluding Missouri, Louisiana, and Arkansas. In 1875, Marshal Fagan hired Reeves as a deputy marshal, making him the first Black deputy to serve west of the Mississippi River.

Reeves spent the next thirty-two years in service as a U.S. marshal dedicated to law and order. He was a man of many talents and impeccable moral character who took his job very seriously. Once he even arrested his own son, Ben "Bennie" Reeves, for the murder of Bennie's wife. Bass Reeves refused to task another marshal with bringing his fugitive son to justice. Once apprehended by his father, Bennie was tried, convicted of murder, and sentenced to eleven years in prison.

Although Bass Reeves was born into legalized chattel slavery, once free he used his skills and talents to enforce American laws. He dedicated his life to law enforcement, and at sixty-nine years old he became a police officer in Oklahoma's Muskogee Police Department for a few years before retiring. He died of Bright's disease in 1910. He was seventy-two years old.

A century after his death, Bass Reeves's incredible story has been immortalized in TV series including *Lawmen: Bass Reeves* and *Watchmen*. Both capture Reeves's larger-than-life persona and unconventional sleuthing, and his unshakable bravery in pursuit of the fugitives of all races whom he brought to justice.

LET'S THINK ABOUT THIS

1. How did Marshal Reeves feel about having the authority to arrest outlaws and criminals—of all races—and bring them to justice?

2. How does the fact that John Brown was white affect his legacy?

3. What do you think life was like for the Black Exodusters who settled in the western territories?

CHAPTER 3

A NATION DIVIDED ON THE ISSUE OF SLAVERY

Turn on any television news channel covering American politics today, and journalists and political pundits will undoubtedly be discussing Democratic and Republican Party views on important issues. In recent years some presidential hopefuls have represented smaller parties such as the Green, Libertarian, or People's Party, but none have ever won enough votes to be real competition for Democratic and Republican candidates.

This wasn't the case in the early years of the nation's history through the mid-nineteenth century, leading up to the Civil War. Back then there were multiple political parties that represented unique and specific viewpoints of their respective constituent voters. Some were more focused on states' rights, while others wanted more federal oversight in government. Prior to the Civil War, each political party had its own stance on the issue of slavery.

American political parties are almost as old as the United States itself. As the Founding Fathers were framing the United States Constitution, political factions developed among leaders with differing ideas about how the burgeoning country should be run and by whom, as well as who qualified as American citizens. Out of these factions grew the two earliest political parties: Alexander Hamilton's Federalist Party was popular in Northern and mid-Atlantic states and the Democratic-Republican Party (also called Jefferson's Republican Party) was popular in Southern and Southeastern states.

Both parties grappled with the issue of slavery from the very start. While Alexander Hamilton opposed slavery, other Federalist leaders like James Madison supported it. Hamilton and the Federalists favored more federal government involvement at the state level and investments in technological innovation instead of the agricultural economy favored in the South. The early Democratic-Republican Party favored states' rights to self-govern and make their own laws, limited oversight by the federal government, and an agricultural economy that boded well for Southern slave owners. It's important to remember that Southern states had grown rich from rice, cotton, tobacco, and indigo crops tilled by enslaved people working on plantations there. Democratic-Republican leaders representing wealthy Southern planters wanted to guarantee protection and continued prosperity for the South and slave culture.

ABRAHAM LINCOLN

In the years leading up to the Civil War, every American politician seeking election had a stance on slavery. Abraham Lincoln was one of them. A self-taught attorney and eloquent speaker, Lincoln was also a savvy anti-slavery proponent whom political opponents never saw coming. Born of humble means in Kentucky, Lincoln was raised in Illinois, where his father moved the family for better work opportunities. Because his father moved the family around quite often, young Abe Lincoln didn't have much formal education growing up. What he did have was a strong work ethic; as a young man, he worked on a riverboat, as a shopkeeper, and as a postmaster before setting his sights on politics.

Henry Clay's Whig Party appealed to Lincoln because of its commitment to helping citizens meet their needs and its goals to spur economic and business development by establishing a national bank and constructing canals, highways, and railroad systems. Lincoln joined the party and ran for Congress as a Whig candidate, and he won! However, Lincoln quickly realized that winning an election was easier than maintaining the support of the people who had elected him.

His staunch criticism of the Mexican-American War, which he viewed as a political scheme to expand slavery farther south, angered his Illinois constituents. Although Illinois had been admitted as a free state in 1818, the state constitution enacted that same year allowed current slave owners to retain their slaves and limited the rights of free Blacks living there. After just one tumultuous term as a congressman, Lincoln did not seek re-election.

At that point in his political career Lincoln wasn't actually an abolitionist (yet), but as a Whig Party member he refused to endorse legislation that condemned abolitionist societies.

Although he had an unremarkable start to his

political career, Lincoln did not let that stop him from shining a light on the pressing need to end slavery. When Stephen Douglas's Kansas-Nebraska Act was passed in 1854, Lincoln was moved to jump back into the political fray in opposition to the possible spread of slavery into the new territory. Using his political platform, Lincoln invoked the tenets of the Declaration of Independence as his arguments against the institution of slavery.

Lincoln eventually left the Whig Party to join the new Republican Party, which opposed slavery as well. He was making a political name for himself.

In several debates during that Senate campaign, Lincoln sparred against Stephen "Little Giant" Douglas—who, remember, was also known for his gift of speaking on the topic of slavery. As orators, the two men were evenly matched. But in politics Lincoln was outmatched by more seasoned political opponents and those within his own party.

That all changed

A campaign button for Abraham Lincoln in the 1860 presidential election.

in 1860, when the Republican Party chose Lincoln as its presidential candidate. Though he had very little political success, he had impressed his party with his electrifying speeches. But becoming the party candidate was one thing; winning the general election was something different.

This time Lincoln was debating not only Douglas, who was running against him as the Northern Democratic candidate, but also two other candidates: John C. Breckenridge, the Southern Democratic candidate, and John Bell, the Constitutional Union Party candidate. It was a four-way race!

As luck would have it, Breckenridge and Bell split the votes in the Southern states, and Lincoln carried the North and the Electoral College to win the presidential election. Lincoln's unlikely victory was a historic win that sent shock waves throughout the South.

The revelation that the sixteenth commander in chief of the United States was a Northern anti-slavery proponent sent Southern political leaders reeling, and by the time President Lincoln was inaugurated in March 1861, South Carolina, Mississippi, Alabama, Georgia, Florida, Louisiana, and Texas had seceded, or declared they were no longer a part of the United States of America, creating the Confederate States of America. Later that year, Virginia, Arkansas, North Carolina, and Tennessee joined the Confederacy.

It's true. Southern states declared that their right to own slaves was more important than having a unified nation. They created their own government and constitution, appointed their own leaders, and refused to acknowledge the legitimacy of Abraham Lincoln as their president.

Today, it may be unfathomable that Southern Americans would start their own country (or even try to), but that's exactly what they did. To be certain they'd be recognized as a legitimate self-governing nation, they needed a president to govern and lead growing secession efforts. The men (and only the men, because women couldn't vote) of the Confederate States of America elected Jefferson Finis Davis as its first and only president.

Jefferson Davis was a Southern statesman, politician, cotton planter, military veteran, and owner of enslaved people. Davis was born in Kentucky but reared in Mississippi, and he represented Mississippi in the U.S. House of Representatives for two terms (1847–1851 and 1857–1861) and was a staunch defender of states' rights to permit, support, and maintain slavery as their way of life. Davis was also a white supremacist who believed that slavery was natural because Blacks were unequal to white people.

He believed so deeply that Southern states had the right to preserve the institution of slavery that he resigned from the U.S. Senate when his home state of Mississippi seceded from the Union. Davis returned to Mississippi in hopes of leading a Confederate military command. Instead, on February 9, 1861, he was elected as pro tempore, or temporary, president of the Confederate States of America, not the job he had had in mind!

Later that year, on November 6, President Jefferson Davis was elected for a six-year term. Davis wanted to be involved in the military action, so he decided that all military operations had to go through him. Davis had been a military cadet at the U.S. Military Academy at West Point, and he fought in the 1832 Black Hawk War, which claimed the lives of over six hundred Sauk, Fox, and Kickapoo Indigenous people in Illinois. But even with relatively little military experience, Davis believed he was qualified to direct the Confederate Army's strategies and tactics. By the end of the Civil War, it was clear that he was wrong.

SHOTS FIRED!

On April 2, 1861, Confederate troops fired shots at the United States military advancing to provide food and provisions to the soldiers stationed at Fort

Sumter, a tactical location in the harbor of Charleston, South Carolina. The Confederates believed the U.S. military might be sending cannons and other ammunition to defend the fort. The incident was the first of many skirmishes in the Civil War, which lasted four years, ending on May 13, 1865. In the end, the Union Army was victorious, defeating the Confederate Army. But the victory was hard-fought and was due to several factors that gave the North the military advantage.

War is costly; it costs in lives lost as well as the economic costs to fund military operations. The Union Army was backed by the financial wealth of Northern states. Unlike the Southern states, which still had an agricultural lifestyle and economy fueled by enslaved people, the Northern states had embraced innovation in transportation and industrialization as a way to make money. The North had some of the first railway systems, which allowed them to transport soldiers and weapons to their troops on the front lines of the war. They also had large factories where American workers mass-produced weapons and artillery for Union soldiers. And the Union had a better navy, which helped it seize and control important Southern waterways like the Mississippi River.

The Union also had two strategic leaders who worked together to cripple the Confederate opposition: President Lincoln and General Ulysses S. Grant. The combination of President Lincoln's diplomatic, economic, and political initiatives and General Grant's military strategies led to the Union's eventual victory in the war.

THE EMANCIPATION PROCLAMATION

Many people believe that when President Lincoln signed the Emancipation Proclamation on January 1, 1863, all enslaved people were given their freedom. That's not entirely true. It applied to "all persons held as slaves" in those states that had seceded from the nation. That was roughly 3.5 million enslaved men, women, and children, but not the five hundred thousand living in border states.

Of course, the Confederate states didn't free their slaves, since they no longer recognized Lincoln as their president. That meant freedom for enslaved people in those states depended on the Union winning the war.

Additionally, when Lincoln signed the Emancipation Proclamation, it was just a wartime order, not a law. That meant another president could overturn the order, or it could be reversed by Congress or a court ruling. To ensure that newly freed slaves remained permanently free, Lincoln's proclamation had to be made law through a constitutional amendment. Constitutional amendments are changes to the United States Constitution, beginning with the Bill of Rights. Each amendment includes specific legal guidelines and provisions for American citizens that must be enforced by the federal government.

As you can imagine, getting an amendment to end slavery passed was not an easy thing to do! To date there have only been twenty-seven amendments, including the Bill of Rights, which was added in 1791. The country was embroiled in a bitter war with itself over the very topic of slavery. Americans living in the South and the North were divided over slavery.

For an amendment to become part of the Constitution, either it must be passed by two-thirds majorities of both the House and Senate or it must be proposed by a convention of two-thirds of the state legislatures. It must then be ratified (approved) by three-quarters of the state legislatures. When the amendment went before Congress in April 1864, it failed to get the required two-thirds majority in the House of Representatives.

Later that year Lincoln was re-elected for a second term. With renewed vigor and determination to end slavery, he persuaded Democrats who had originally voted against the amendment and those who had not cast a vote to have a change of heart and vote in favor of what became the Thirteenth Amendment.

The Thirteenth Amendment was finally passed on January 31, 1865, and later ratified when the state of Georgia was the twenty-seventh state to approve it.

WATCH NIGHT

With Lincoln's bold move to end slavery once and for all, enslaved and formerly enslaved people experienced newfound hope that a long-held collective dream, passed down from generation to generation, would be realized in their lifetime: freedom. It appeared change was coming, and a new life, free of the shackles of bondage, was on the horizon for millions of Black people in the Southern and border states.

While Union and Confederate soldiers raged against one another in unrelenting battle, enslaved and free African Americans impatiently waited for the new year's arrival. When the clock struck midnight, enslaved people in Union-liberated Confederate states would no longer be somebody's property. The rest would actually see freedom only if and when the Union defeated the Confederate Army, and when that would happen was anybody's guess.

President Lincoln had signed the Emancipation Proclamation on September 22, 1862, and word quickly spread throughout the South. For the very first time many who had never known freedom in their lifetime, or their parents' lifetimes, had hope that they would see it for themselves. They knew emancipation wouldn't go into effect until midnight on January 1, 1863—the start of the new year. That's what made that New Year's Eve so special and gave the night new meaning and promise.

Throughout the Confederate South, enslaved folks gathered to pray, give thanks, and count down to the new year, or the year of jubilee. As they sang and prayed, congregants would ask out loud, "Watchman, watchman, please tell me the hour of the night."

The minister would reply, "It is three minutes to midnight. . . . It is two minutes to midnight. . . . It is one minute to midnight. . . . And now it's midnight. Freedom time has come!" The formerly enslaved people, now newly freed, danced, sang, and shouted in jubilant joy at their freedom.

Enslaved Black people had been practicing their form of Christianity in praise houses, small shacks set off in the woods, and hush harbors, wooden structures made from tree branches arranged in secluded areas away from white people's prying eyes because it was illegal for more than seven Black people to gather, even for religious ceremonies. In those spiritual places, enslaved people found peace and comfort by blending Christianity with African traditions that had been passed down and preserved, such as the ring shout, in which singers dance in a circle singing hymns and clapping. The ring shout comes from West African traditions as a spiritual way to praise and thank God and their ancestors.

It was also in those secret, sacred places that enslaved people devised escape plans and passed along word of uprisings and other anti-slavery information they learned from other enslaved people or by eavesdropping on white people.

So it's not surprising that they would gather in church to usher in their collective Jubilee Day (the day an enslaved person got their freedom) and celebrate their newfound freedom.

In many Black churches across the U.S., Watch Night or Freedom's Eve services are still observed on New Year's Eve. This tradition remains as a custom passed down from generation to generation in collective memory of how God kept his promise to their ancestors. Watch Night is a cultural ritual that connects the present with the past and symbolizes Christian hope, faith, and deliverance. Later, on New Year's Day, many African Americans celebrate the new year with traditional soul-food meals that include collard greens, hoppin' John, corn bread, and ham.

THE CONTRIBUTIONS OF BLACK SOLDIERS

When Lincoln issued the Emancipation Proclamation, he galvanized Union soldiers around a very specific military objective. Fighting to end slavery appealed to Black men, of course, many of whom knew first-hand the devastation of enslavement. At the urging of Black leaders like Frederick Douglass, President Lincoln opened military service to Black men. Secretary of War Edwin M. Stanton approved all-Black regiments to support Union efforts. Although they would be fighting to save the Union, some Northern whites didn't like the idea of Blacks being armed with weapons, even if it was in their defense. Others didn't believe Black soldiers were fit to fight at all.

By the war's end, two hundred thousand Black men had enlisted in the United States Army and Navy. As Black Union soldiers, they followed a path laid by Black patriots such as Peter Salem, Cato

Smith, and Crispus Attucks, who had made notable contributions to the American Revolutionary War almost a century before.

Over the course of the last two years of the war, Black soldiers demonstrated valor and courage in fighting, which led to successful Union raids and skirmishes with Confederate forces. The Fifty-Fourth Massachusetts Volunteer Infantry Regiment, the Second South Carolina Volunteer Infantry Regiment, and the Twenty-First United States Colored Troops were a few of the all-Black Civil War regiments.

The Fifty-Fourth Massachusetts wasn't just fighting the Confederate enemy; they also had to battle the racism of military and political leaders who didn't believe Black men were fit for battle. On top of that, this was something that had never been done in such magnitude: assembling and arming Black men alongside white soldiers for battle. In the previous century the First Rhode Island Regiment had been made up of one hundred valiant Indigenous and Black soldiers (many of whom were enslaved) who served in the American Revolutionary War. They were a small but mighty group of brave soldiers who aided the Continental Army (the colonists) in many notable battles against the British, including the Siege of Boston. At the end of the colonial uprising, some of the American Black

An 1863 print showing the Fifty-Fourth Massachusetts Colored Regiment and the death of Colonel Shaw.

fighters gained their freedom, but a great many did not. Interestingly, those who chose to fight alongside the British *were* granted their freedom at the war's end.

Less than a hundred years later, Black men again stood up to fight for America. But there was a big difference: the Fifty-Fourth Massachusetts was ten times larger than the First Rhode Island, and it was composed of Black men whose families had experienced several generations of slavery. The promise of victory meant the end of slavery, not just freedom for themselves, as it had been for those who had fought alongside the patriots decades before. Among the ranks of the Fifty-Fourth were offspring of noted Black abolitionists, including Sergeant Major Lewis

Henry Douglass and 1st Sergeant Charles Remond Douglass, sons of Frederick Douglass; Toussaint L'Ouverture Delany, son of Martin Robison Delany; and James Caldwell, grandson of Sojourner Truth.

Colonel Shaw and the thirty-six other white men who led the regiment of over one thousand Black men fought alongside them against Confederate soldiers at South Carolina's Fort Wagner, overlooking Charleston Harbor. Shaw and his men were the first of the many units to advance toward their Confederate enemies, putting themselves directly in the line of fire. In the face of imminent danger and death, the men trotted toward the fort, undeterred by the cannon fire overhead.

By the time they breached the fort wall, Colonel Shaw had been killed. Valiantly, his men fought on, never letting the Union colors (the flag) fall to the ground as a sign of victory. And they were victorious for a while. Members of the Fifty-Fourth and other soldiers held the fort until they were surrounded and overtaken by Confederate soldiers.

Fifteen hundred American soldiers died that day; Union soldiers made up most of the casualties, while the Confederates lost only 174 men in the melee. The men of the Fifty-Fourth Massachusetts suffered the most, with over six hundred injured or killed.

Confederate soldiers had been livid when they saw Black men fighting alongside white soldiers. The idea that an enslaved or even a free Black person could be allowed to carry weapons to fight against white soldiers enraged them. In a final act of victory and to show disrespect to Colonel Shaw, the Confederate soldiers tossed his battle-worn body into a massive unmarked grave along with the Black men who had died fighting alongside him that day.

They didn't know that Shaw came from a family of abolitionists. Shaw's family saw his death as an honorable ending for his valor in a great cause.

The courage and spirit of the Fifty-Fourth Massachusetts in the face of great losses during the battle at Fort Wagner was captured in the 1989 film *Glory*, starring Academy Award–winning actors Denzel Washington and Morgan Freeman, who played Fifty-Fourth Massachusetts soldiers, and Matthew Broderick, who portrayed Colonel Robert G. Shaw—in real life Shaw trained and led the troops into battle. Although he was killed in the battle and they ultimately lost at Fort Wagner, those who remained standing fought to the bitter end.

BLACK BOYS SERVED IN THE UNION ARMY

The Fifty-Fourth Massachusetts was predominantly made up of young enlisted Black men of no more than twenty-four years old, with some as young as sixteen.

One of the youngest to serve with Company H of the Fifty-Fourth Massachusetts was Miles Moore, a Black youth from Elmira, New York. At just sixteen, Moore served as company drummer alongside Colonel Shaw, who had given the boy the military designation. Alexander H. Johnson was another sixteen-year-old who served alongside the Fifty-Fourth Massachusetts. Johnson played the drum to honor the fallen Colonel Shaw during his funeral. Moore, Johnson, and John Walters, another sixteen-year-old, were the youngest company members of the Fifty-Fourth Massachusetts.

Images of smoky, chaotic battlefields might not conjure the sound of music. However, drumming was an important element of battle during the Civil War.

Drummers in the Union and Confederate armies played a critical role as soldiers marched in time and in unison with the rhythm of the drummers' percussive beats. Drumming directed soldiers' synchronized movements toward the enemy and signaled specific tasks and military tactics that infantrymen (foot soldiers) were ordered to carry out on the battlefield.

Drummers, like chaplains (military clergymen), were considered noncombatants, which means they did not fight or even carry weapons. That didn't mean their job wasn't dangerous!

They marched behind the infantry and were often in the direct line of enemy fire. Many drummers lost their lives. Many of them were children, some even younger than Moore, Johnson, and Walters.

When they weren't keeping time with their drums, drummer boys doubled as medical assistants to doctors who took care of the wounded and even had the grisly job of retrieving dismembered body parts and severed limbs of wounded and fallen soldiers.

THE DANGERS BLACK SOLDIERS FACED

Can you imagine signing up for potentially life-threatening duty to help save the United States from collapse? Well, that's what approximately 1 percent of Americans do when they join one of the nation's military branches today.

Now imagine signing up to fight for the nation and facing racism and pay discrimination from fellow soldiers and military leaders. That's what nearly two hundred thousand Black Union soldiers experienced when they began volunteering for service in 1862. As the numbers of Black volunteers swelled, Congress created the Bureau of Colored Troops to manage newly enlisted Blacks, who held many different jobs, including cooks, laborers, scouts, nurses, chaplains, steamboat pilots, and infantry.

Yet even with all their contributions, Black Union volunteers were not fully appreciated or compensated for their work. For example, Black soldiers were paid ten dollars per month—the equivalent of $325 today—with three dollars deducted for their uniforms, while white soldiers were paid thirteen dollars per month with no deduction for uniforms. It would take two years before Congress addressed this injustice in 1864 and granted equal pay to the U.S. Colored Troops, including retroactive pay.

Black troops who were captured and taken as prisoners of war by the Confederate Army also endured more violence and physical torture than white Union prisoners. In 1864, in one of the most egregiously violent incidents on record, Confederate soldiers executed Black soldiers they captured after a battle at Fort Pillow, Tennessee. Confederate Army leaders witnessed the killings but didn't stop the soldiers. Confederate Major General Nathan Forrest led the deadly assault on the mostly Black Union soldiers. After the war, Forrest used his role as the first grand wizard of the Ku Klux Klan to terrorize free Blacks.

On top of the discrimination and threat of torture and death at the hands of the Confederate Army, many Black Civil War veterans never received their military pensions, which should have been a guaranteed lifelong payment that comes with military service.

HARRIET THE SPY

Down South, behind enemy lines, Harriet Tubman led 150 men in the Combahee Ferry Raid, freeing over seven hundred enslaved men, women, and children.

You may know Tubman as the fearless abolitionist and one of the conductors of the Underground Railroad, but she was also a Union spy and the only woman to lead a military expedition during the war. In 1863 Tubman led Union Colonel James Montgomery and his men in a raid of rice plantations along the Combahee River.

Tubman and other Black people—free, enslaved, and fugitive slaves—were valued intelligence agents who snuck behind enemy lines and gathered tactical information and details about their plans, where they

An 1868 woodcut depicting Harriet Tubman.

stored weapons, and any prisoners of war they had. Each time they relayed information, they risked their lives and their freedom. The messages they offered Union leaders were called "black dispatches."

Harriet Tubman served as a nurse, cook, spy, and scout, but the United States repeatedly denied her request for a veteran's pension for her honorable and considerable military service. As was the case for many Black veterans who were denied their rightful benefits due to administrative errors or other bureaucratic problems, it would take thirty-seven years for Tubman to receive a portion of the pension she was owed. When she was finally awarded that, it was a "widow's pension" resulting from her second husband's military service, not for her own contributions.

Notable Black Members of the United States Armed Forces

Black men and women didn't only fight for the Union Army in the Civil War. They've been an important part of the military since the country's founding. Their service and expertise have led to many U.S. military victories. Here are a few of the most notable Black service members from our history:

- James Armistead, working for the Marquis de Lafayette, was a spy in the Continental Army during the American Revolutionary War.
- Benjamin O. Davis Sr. was the first African American brigadier general in the United States Army, promoted in 1940.
- The Tuskegee Airmen were the first Black military airmen, who piloted more than fifteen thousand sorties (wartime combat flights) between 1941 and 1943 during World War II. They lost the fewest escort fighter aircraft (planes that accompanied aircraft carrying bombs) of any unit and were in demand for service by the Allied bomb units.
- Benjamin O. Davis Jr., the son of Brigadier

General Benjamin O. Davis Sr., was a decorated pilot and commander in the United States Army before transferring to the Army Air Corps (now the United States Air Force) in 1942. In 1998, Benjamin O. Davis Jr. was promoted to general in the USAF.

- Also during World War II, the 6888th Central Postal Directory Battalion, the only all-female, predominantly African American unit, was assigned to posts in England and France. Their task was to process the backlog of undelivered mail during the war.

- Carl Maxie Brashear was a U.S. Navy sailor who rose to the rank of master diver. Brashear served from 1948 to 1979, and his story was featured in the movie *Men of Honor.*

- Air Force General Daniel "Chappie" James Jr. became the first African American four-star general in 1975.

- Captain Theresa Claiborne was the first Black woman pilot to fly in the United States Air Force, in 1982. Captain Claiborne went on to become the first Black woman in the U.S. Air Force to serve as a command pilot and instructor for the KC-135, a plane that refuels other aircraft in midair.

- General Colin Powell was a four-star general in the U.S. Army and later U.S. secretary of state, appointed in 2001.
- In 2022, U.S. Marine Corps General Michael E. Langley became the first Black four-star general in the history of the Marines.
- General Charles Q. Brown was the first African American to serve as chair of the Joint Chiefs of Staff in 2023.

THE BATTLE OF GETTYSBURG

The Battle of Gettysburg was fought over three days at Gettysburg, Pennsylvania. When it was over, the Union had gained the strategic advantage over General Robert E. Lee's Confederate troops.

For most of the battle, Confederate troops dominated Union soldiers. Against the odds, General Lee's men had defeated the Union in the intense Battle of Chancellorsville, Virginia, not long before, with half as many soldiers. With such an unlikely win under his belt, Lee was confident that his troops could overcome the Union Army at Gettysburg, despite it being so far away from the South.

On July 1 the Confederates boldly advanced toward Gettysburg and subdued the twenty thousand soldiers they encountered, forcing Union soldiers to turn back.

On July 2 both sides continued the fight, resulting in mass casualties. General Lee remained optimistic about their ability to end the fight in yet another victory. But Union Army commander Major General Winfield S. Hancock and other leaders were able to keep Lee and his men at bay.

On July 3 Confederate soldiers totaling close to thirteen thousand advanced upon the Union. Believing their enemy was weak, Brigadier General George E. Pickett boldly led half of those Confederate soldiers as they charged over a one-mile ridge to overwhelm and overtake Union soldiers positioned there. They were met with fierce resistance and opposition they had not anticipated from Union troops half their number. Confederate soldiers were bombarded by cannon and artillery fire as they charged toward Union soldiers. Though weakened by fire, the Union soldiers descended upon Lee's troops.

Both Lee and Pickett had underestimated the Union troops, who defended their tactical position on the ridge and subdued the Confederate offense. Pickett's overconfidence had cost the lives of more than half of his men.

For three days, military leaders on both sides had tried different strategies to get the upper hand in the bloody battle. But when the fighting had ended and the gun smoke had cleared, forty-five thousand American soldiers were dead, injured, captured, or missing, all casualties of America's war with itself.

Although fighting continued for another two years after the Battle of Gettysburg, the bloody loss weakened the Confederate Army and signaled a turning point in the war.

Four months after the Battle of Gettysburg, on November 19, 1863, President Lincoln gave one of the most compelling speeches of his presidency. You might recognize the famous opening lines: "Fourscore and seven years ago our fathers brought forth, on this continent, a new nation." The speech is a mere 272 words long and lasted only a few short minutes.

Lincoln delivered the speech at the dedication of a military cemetery in Gettysburg to honor the soldiers who had died there. The brief speech is a powerful admonishment of the Confederacy's continued efforts to fight and win the war. For Lincoln, the goals of the war were clear: save the Union and maintain democracy at all costs. And although he had made abolition the prize of a Union victory, he didn't mention it at all in his memorial to the fallen soldiers who died fighting over the issue of slavery:

Fourscore and seven years ago our fathers brought forth, on this continent, a new nation, conceived in liberty, and dedicated to the proposition that all men are created equal.

Now we are engaged in a great civil war, testing whether that nation, or any nation so conceived, and so dedicated, can long endure. We are met on a great battle-field of that war. We have come to dedicate a portion of that field, as a final resting-place for those who here gave their lives, that that nation might live. It is altogether fitting and proper that we should do this.

But, in a larger sense, we cannot dedicate, we cannot consecrate—we cannot hallow—this ground. The brave men, living and dead, who struggled here, have consecrated it, far above our poor power to add or detract. The world will little note, nor long remember what we say here, but it can never forget what they did here. It is for us the living, rather, to be dedicated here to the unfinished work which they who fought here have thus far so

nobly advanced. It is rather for us to be here dedi-
cated to the great task remaining before us—that
from these honored dead we take increased devotion
to that cause for which they gave the last full measure
of devotion—that we here highly resolve that these
dead shall not have died in vain—that this nation,
under God, shall have a new birth of freedom, and
that government of the people, by the people, for the
people, shall not perish from the earth.

UNION VICTORY

The Civil War ended on April 9, 1865, with the surrender of General Lee to General Grant at Appomat-
tox Court House, Virginia. General Lee's soldiers in
the Confederate Army of Virginia were outmanned
and outmaneuvered by General Grant's Union soldiers. By the end of the war, the Confederate Army
was low on food, supplies, and men due to desertion
by battle-weary soldiers and war casualties.

General Grant had offered General Lee the option
of surrender on several occasions, but despite mounting setbacks, Lee had pressed on.

They had nowhere to go, because the Union soldiers had them surrounded. Eventually, General Lee

accepted Grant's terms for his surrender. A month later, Jefferson Davis, the president of the Confederate States, was captured and charged with treason for his leadership in the Confederacy, although he never actually went to trial for his part in the secession from the Union.

General Lee's surrender, the capture of Jefferson Davis, and the capture and surrender of the remaining Confederate troops put the final nails in the Confederate States' coffin.

The Civil War was the nation's deadliest war. Until very recently the estimated number of casualties was almost 620,000, with 360,000 Union soldiers and 258,000 Confederate soldiers lost. Earlier estimates were made by Union veterans who scoured census reports, military rolls, cemetery records, and other vital records (like birth and death certificates) to identify how many men had lost their lives during the war. They also accounted for boys and men who went "missing" during the war, meaning there were records of their births but no records of their deaths. The documented deaths of soldiers plus the numbers of missing boys and men equaled the long-held estimation of 620,000 Civil War casualties. In 1900, Thomas Leonard Livermore, one of the veterans who set out to document the war's death toll, published *Numbers and Losses in the Civil War in America, 1861–65,* which reveals his findings.

However, new research of census data on young men during the war suggests the number of lives lost is actually somewhere between 650,000 and 850,000. In 2011 Dr. J. David Hacker, a demographic historian, or history scholar who studies population growth and decline in a specific span of time, re-evaluated census data and vital records of the decades between 1850 and 1870. But Hacker went further than Livermore and the other Union veterans who tried to figure out how many soldiers had lost their lives in the Civil War conflict, by studying birth and death patterns of men and boys in specific regions between 1850 and 1870. Hacker's new approach to the census data revealed that a significant reduction—nearly 23 percent—in the South's population of young males was due to the Civil War.

Well over half a million—perhaps closer to a million—Americans lost their lives fighting a war that was, at its core, about white Southerners' belief that they had the right to own human beings and use their free labor to support their way of life.

PRESIDENT LINCOLN ASSASSINATED

President Lincoln was largely responsible for ending slavery and the civil war that had fractured the nation for over four years. By the time of his presidency, the nation was deeply divided over the issue of slavery. Recent legislation like the Kansas-Nebraska Act and the 1850 Fugitive Slave Act had made the 1850s tumultuous times and 1860 a volatile year to be elected president of the United States of America.

Although Lincoln was not a pro-slavery politician, the abolition of slavery wasn't always a presidential priority for him. But when Southern leaders seceded and formed the Confederate States of America, largely over what they believed was a right to own slaves and self-govern with little to no federal interference, he embraced abolition as a way to cripple the Southern economy and stop the growing troubles that threatened the American republic. Over time, interactions with abolitionists strengthened his commitment to abolition and his belief that it was the right thing to do for the country. He even changed his stance, from believing that freed slaves should be sent "back" to Africa to advocating for resources and protections under the law for the newly freed population here in

America. His signing of the Emancipation Proclamation was a radical act of abolition and social justice that changed the course of the nation.

Sadly, he did not live long enough to see the fruits of his presidential leadership materialize. He was shot on April 14, 1865, by John Wilkes Booth, just days after the surrender of the Confederacy, while attending a performance at Ford's Theatre in Washington, D.C. He died the next day.

Booth came from a famous family of actors, and he himself was known for his "stage presence" and command of the audience. He was also a proponent of slavery who was aggrieved by General Lee's surrender and the fall of the Confederacy. He wanted to do something about the devastating blow the South had experienced at the hands of the Union Army and President Lincoln.

He enlisted the help of other Confederate enthusiasts and devised plans to kill Lincoln, as well as Vice President Andrew Johnson and Secretary of State William Seward, who were second and third in line for the presidency in the event of Lincoln's death.

The planned attack on Johnson never happened, and the attack on Seward left him permanently scarred but alive after Booth's co-conspirator broke into his home and slashed him with a knife repeatedly.

For his part, Booth carried out his assassination of Lincoln as if it were a theatrical production. He barged into the theater box where Lincoln, his wife, and their guests were seated, and just as there was a crescendo of laughter at the show, he shot the president in the back of the head before leaping down onto the stage.

Landing on the stage, Booth broke his leg and is rumored to have shouted, "The South is avenged!" Other witnesses claimed he shouted, "Sic semper tyrannis," the motto of the state of Virginia, which means "Thus always to tyrants."

Booth escaped Ford's Theatre and avoided capture for twelve days. On April 26, 1865, he was finally found, along with one of his co-conspirators. When he refused to surrender for his crime, Booth was shot and killed on a farm near Virginia's Rappahannock River.

● ● ●

Decoration Day, the First Memorial Day

Here in the United States, Memorial Day is a national holiday to remember and honor the lives of

American service members who have lost their lives in battle, and it's also the unofficial start to summer. From coast to coast, Americans gather at barbecues and local parades and, depending upon where they live, may look to the sky for spectacular fireworks displays or death-defying aviation stunts by some of the best American military pilots.

Each year Memorial Day is commemorated by people from all walks of life. It wasn't a national holiday until 1971, but by that time, Americans had already been holding what was then called Decoration Day ceremonies and parades for over a hundred years! On May 1, 1865, newly freed African Americans in Charleston, South Carolina, gathered the remains of fallen Union soldiers that had been left in a mass grave. To memorialize the soldiers' sacrifices, they reburied them and decorated the graves with flowers. They called it Decoration Day, and it is recognized as the very first Memorial Day.

Three years later, General John A. Logan, who had been a successful military leader in the Union Army, initiated a movement to set aside a day each year to honor Union soldiers who had lost their lives in the Civil War. Through his organization, the Grand Army of the Republic, Logan rallied Americans everywhere to set aside May 30, 1868, as a day to pay homage to fallen Civil War soldiers by decorating their graves. Logan's wife had witnessed how the graves of fallen Confederate soldiers had been adorned with flowers while she was on a spring trip to Virginia. After hearing how moved his wife had been at the sight of the decorated graves, Logan was inspired to do the same for fallen Union soldiers. We can't say for sure why he picked May 30, but maybe it was because it coincides with Confederate Memorial Day, which remains an official state holiday in Mississippi, Alabama, and South Carolina.

Logan's journey to being recognized as the founder of Memorial Day is a storied one. Born in Jackson County, Illinois, Logan seemed destined to follow in his father's political footsteps. John Logan Sr. had been a Democratic leader in Illinois government and a slave owner. As a young man, his son also supported the institution of slavery and believed enslavement was a fitting way of life for Black people. But when the Civil War broke out, Logan made an unpredictable decision: He joined the Union Army, even though he was pro-slavery. Logan chose his country over his party.

Logan served valiantly and led the Union through

numerous battles. During combat he had a change of heart about slavery after seeing the conditions of enslaved people throughout the South. When the war ended, General Logan became a vocal supporter of the newly freed and all Black people, of women's suffrage, and of the recognition of all fallen Civil War soldiers.

In 1971, Congress signed into law the Uniform Monday Holiday Act, which moved several federal holidays to Mondays so working Americans would have long weekends throughout the year. Since then, Memorial Day, which honors not only the estimated 620,000 to 850,000 American soldiers who perished during the Civil War but all service members who have lost their lives defending our nation and allies, has been observed on the last Monday of May.

● ● ●

JUNETEENTH

In 2021 President Joe Biden signed a bill to make Juneteenth a federal holiday. Juneteenth commemorates the June 19, 1865, date when African Americans enslaved in Texas were finally liberated by Union soldiers—two years *after* President Lincoln signed the Emancipation Proclamation and two months after the end of the war.

Texas was one of the Confederate states that had seceded from the United States. Although Lincoln's order freed all enslaved people held captive in Confederate-controlled states, Confederate leaders refused to honor the presidential decree because after seceding, they no longer recognized the president of the United States of America as their leader.

And since slavery had been the most important political issue that drove their decisions to leave the Union and declare war, Texas slave owners weren't in any rush to free their slaves. In June 1865, Major General George Granger and two thousand Union soldiers arrived in Galveston, Texas, to end the Civil War, welcome Texas back into the Union, and inform the more than two hundred thousand enslaved African Americans there that they were finally freed.

Newly freed African Americans marked their liberation in communal celebrations dubbed "Juneteenth," and African Americans in Texas have continued honoring the anniversary with parades, picnics, and festivals. Since then, African Americans living in other parts of the country have also set aside Juneteenth to memorialize the emancipation of their

An Emancipation Day, or Juneteenth,
parade in Richmond, VA in 1905.

ancestors and pay homage to their perseverance and contributions to the country.

While Juneteenth is now a national holiday, not all states recognize it as a state holiday. That means in some states, government offices remain open and state employees do not get the day off. Even so, millions of Americans celebrate Juneteenth to honor the end of slavery once and for all and to mark a new chapter in United States history. That new chapter was focused on rebuilding the fractured nation. It was called the Reconstruction era.

LET'S THINK ABOUT THIS

1. The Constitution does not require presidential signatures on amendments, but Lincoln added his, making it the only constitutional amendment to be later ratified that was signed by a president. Why did President Lincoln sign the Thirteenth Amendment anyway?

2. Why did the newly freed African Americans feel moved to rebury and honor the dead Union soldiers at the end of the Civil War?

3. What do you think was the first thing newly freed African Americans did once they were free? Where do you think they went? What, if anything, did they take with them?

CHAPTER 4

ABOLITION OFF
THE BATTLEFIELD

As the Civil War threatened to break out, political and community leaders were considering what a post-slavery America might look like. Some believed the country and a future newly freed Black population might be better off if formerly enslaved people left the United States altogether.

"Back to Africa" movements began as early as the late 1700s, when the British established Sierra Leone as a "Province of Freedom," a colony for free and formerly enslaved Blacks who fought for the British monarchy during the American Revolution. Since that time, there have been numerous African American leaders who promoted moving to Africa as a viable option for those seeking acceptance, liberation, and opportunities for prosperity.

Beginning in the early 1800s, white people—including some influential politicians like James Monroe and Andrew Jackson, who would go on to be U.S. presidents—began working to devise a way to send Black people "back" to Africa. The irony of the movement to repatriate (send someone back to their original country) Black people to Africa was that by that time, most of them had been born in the United States. Once again Black people would be strangers in a strange land.

Due to poor recordkeeping, it was virtually impossible to know where every captive African and their American-born offspring had originated. Nevertheless, the idea appealed to many whites and some free Blacks, and it grew into a movement that spanned several decades leading up to and even during the Civil War.

Martin Robison Delany was an abolitionist, politician, writer, and Union Army veteran. He is regarded by many as the father of "Black nationalism," the belief that Black people should be free and self-determining, and for some, the belief that they should live separately in their own nation. He traveled to Liberia, in West Africa, in 1859, and his experience sparked a desire to start a colony for Black people there. But when he was unable to purchase land there, Delany threw his efforts behind abolition in his homeland.

When the Civil War started, Delany enlisted to fight alongside Union soldiers and rallied Black men to join the Union Army. For his valor, Delany was promoted to major in 1865. After he made a great impression on President Abraham Lincoln, the president appointed him to be the first Black field officer. Fighting as Union soldiers was the ultimate way Delany and other Black men fought for the abolition of slavery.

Some Black abolitionists considered going to Central America in search of opportunities, because they had little hope of acceptance as full American citizens by whites. Lewis Douglass, abolitionist, Union soldier, and son of the famed abolitionist Frederick Douglass, was one of them. Lewis saw the promise of opportunity for himself in Linconia, a colony in what is now Panama that President Lincoln wanted to establish for free and newly emancipated Blacks. Frederick Douglass, however, didn't buy into colonization plans developed for Black people by whites, because they were rooted in racism and white supremacist notions of Black inferiority. For the elder Douglass, if Black

Frederick Douglass was the most photographed person in the nineteenth century! He sat for 160 photos and portraits during his life, including this one from 1864. Douglass believed being photographed raised his profile as a person of influence.

people wanted to leave the only homeland they had ever known in search of better work and education options, that was one thing. But if they were moved to all-Black colonies established by white people who felt Blacks were inferior, well, that was another thing entirely, and not something Frederick Douglass could support.

Even though Douglass didn't agree with the premise behind Linconia, he supported his son's decision to join five hundred other free Blacks in the Panamanian colony. In the end, Lincoln's plans fell through, and Lewis and the other African Americans never moved to Panama. But the seeds of repatriation and expatriation had been planted, and as time went on, other Blacks considered leaving the United States and eventually did so. Some went to places in Africa, but others to Europe and other parts of the world in search of acceptance and opportunities.

Later, in the twentieth century, a radical Jamaican-born Black leader by the name of Marcus Mosiah Garvey Jr. would advocate for African American separatism (meaning living apart from white people) and began a campaign to encourage formerly enslaved people and their descendants to move to Liberia, where he hoped to establish a community.

While Garvey's dream of establishing new Black colonies in Liberia never fully took hold, by the late twentieth century African Americans had begun moving to areas throughout West Africa, including Ghana and Liberia. In 2019 Ghana planned a year-long initiative called the Year of Return, to encourage African Americans to visit and move to the West African nation to mark the four-hundred-year anniversary of the 1619 arrival of the first captured Africans to Jamestown, Virginia.

By 2023, fifteen hundred African Americans had heeded the invitation and moved to Ghana to start their lives in the motherland.

WILLIAM LLOYD GARRISON

By the 1800s, advances in printing presses had led to a major boom in publishing in the United States and around the world. The number of American newspapers and mercantile (a fancy way to describe trade in or the sale of goods, items, and at that time, people) publications increased as rapidly as the nation's growth in population and new territories. At first, reading newspapers and mercantile magazines was a luxury reserved for rich white people. That's because rich people were more often than not literate, while poor whites, like slaves, were mostly illiterate. But by the mid-1800s more of the American population was literate, including free and enslaved Blacks who secretly learned to read and write.

As more people began reading, the demand for books and newspapers grew. Activists on both sides of the slavery issue seized upon the publishing industry to voice their arguments for or against slavery.

Abolitionists William Lloyd Garrison and Frederick Douglass published newspapers to encourage citizens to fight for abolition. For over thirty years Garrison published the *Liberator,* which was the most popular anti-slavery periodical of the time. A devout

Christian, Garrison saw slavery as a moral issue. In the nascent years of his abolition work, he supported the idea of sending freed slaves back to Africa. However, over time he rejected this ideology and embraced the idea of "immediate emancipation." Advocates of immediate emancipation believed the best abolition strategy meant putting an immediate end to the entire system of slavery and then incorporating free Black people into society as equal citizens. It was a radical idea for many, even those who wanted slavery to end.

That's because not all abolitionists were alike. Some didn't want slavery to spread to new American territories. These were the "Free-Soilers," who only focused on stopping the legalization of slavery in the newly acquired Indigenous territory. Others were "colonizationists," who supported the idea of deporting newly emancipated Black people. Still others opposed the idea of slavery but had no idea what abolition might mean for formerly enslaved people or the country. These people were abolitionists in theory only.

Garrison's embrace of immediate emancipation reflected his growing radicalism. He founded the New England Anti-Slavery Society in 1832 and helped to establish the American Anti-Slavery Society in 1833, both focused on immediate emancipation.

When he became frustrated with the slow pace of abolition, Garrison embraced even more extreme views. Garrison saw Christian perfectionism as the only way to end slavery, and he denounced the Church and any government that did not abolish slavery, including the United States government. Garrison's thinking also extended to women, whose participation in activism he fully supported, though it was unpopular at the time.

Fellow activists tolerated Garrison's arguments for perfectionism, but his advocacy for women activists was a bridge too far for many of them. Garrison became increasingly radical; he praised John Brown's violent raid on Harpers Ferry and even burned a copy of the United States Constitution at an abolitionist rally!

It seemed there was no turning back for Garrison. But when the Civil War erupted, he supported President Lincoln, seeing the Emancipation Proclamation as the righteous victory he had worked for.

A FAMILY BUSINESS

The children of William Lloyd Garrison and Frederick Douglass grew up in abolitionist households frequently visited by famous activists and fugitive slaves seeking shelter. Their children were privy to passionate debates and discussions of the best strategies for pressing political leaders to support abolition. The two leaders made instilling abolitionist values in their children a top priority!

When Garrison's oldest son, George Thompson Garrison, was born, the proud father wrote a series of poems dedicated to the boy in which he expressed hope that the baby would grow into a man who hated the injustice of slavery. Becoming a father filled Garrison with pride, but it also gave him a glimpse of what enslaved people felt: the hope and desire to protect their children, which they so often could not do.

George Garrison and his brothers, William Lloyd Garrison Jr., Wendell Phillips Garrison, and Francis Jackson Garrison, grew up to be abolitionists like their father.

The children of Frederick and Anna Murray Douglass began abolitionist work at a young age. They witnessed what abolition activism looked like firsthand and took part in the work, helping their father publish his anti-slavery publication, the *North Star*, by folding the papers and preparing them to be mailed. Later, sons Lewis and Frederick Jr. took over the publishing helm when their father was away speaking.

It shouldn't come as a surprise that both Garrison

and Douglass raised abolitionist children. Garrison's son George enlisted in the Union Army when the Civil War broke out. He served as a second lieutenant for the Fifty-Fifth Massachusetts Infantry. Wendell Garrison was an advocate for Black education and voting rights; he wielded his influence to expose lynchings and other terror tactics used to oppress free Blacks during Reconstruction. After the Civil War ended, George Garrison and Charles Douglass turned their activism to securing protections for the Black population.

The Garrisons and the Douglasses were not unique abolitionist families. Abolition was a family cause in most instances. Take Harriet Tubman as another example. Although she never had children, some of her relatives worked with her in the Underground Railroad, including her uncle and cousins.

Children, white and Black, whose parents were actively involved in the Underground Railroad did their parts to shelter runaways. They helped provide food to tired, hungry, and thirsty houseguests. More important, they were great secret keepers, never letting on that their families were harboring fugitive slaves.

On many occasions the Garrison and Douglass children did what they could to comfort and certainly conceal scared runaways. And when famous and even eccentric abolitionists like John Brown came to town, they learned all about the anti-slavery cause. They were children, but growing up in an abolitionist home meant being involved with risky adult business sometimes!

ANNA MURRAY DOUGLASS

Anna Murray Douglass, the first wife of Frederick Douglass, stayed out of the limelight but also played an important role in abolition. Murray Douglass was born free on Maryland's Eastern Shore. Even before meeting Frederick Bailey (Douglass's given surname before he changed it) and helping him escape slavery by sewing a sailor uniform as his disguise, she had worked with the Underground Railroad to assist runaways making their way to free states.

Throughout their nearly forty-five-year marriage, Murray Douglass raised the couple's five children, maintained their home for visiting notable abolitionists, and assisted her husband with publication of his abolitionist paper, the *North Star*.

Unlike her husband, who was a prolific writer and eloquent speaker, Murray Douglass could not read or write. Her illiteracy and dark skin led many Black and white abolitionists to feel she was not suitable for Douglass, whose stature and reputation were recognized throughout the United States and Europe. But the classism and colorism—the belief that lighter-skinned Black people are more physically attractive than those with darker complexions—Murray Douglass experienced cannot diminish the importance of her abolition work, and her abolitionist children credited her influence on their activism in their writing and public speeches.

WHITE ABOLITIONIST FAMILIES

During the nineteenth century, many wealthy white women didn't work outside the home. Lower-class women, however, did work as maids and cooks, and young white women could work as teachers. However, women couldn't be lawyers, politicians, entrepreneurs, or religious leaders. That's because American and British society held very narrow ideas about women's roles and duties. A woman's father, then her husband, and then the home and children were her responsibilities. Women could also teach their children, which more often than not included Bible instruction.

Of course, this standard did not apply to enslaved women, who had no rights to their children or the luxury of caring for them as they saw fit.

Many abolitionist mothers were also Christians, and they used their role as mothers to instill Christian values in their children. They saw abolition as part of their Christian calling and their motherhood. There was even an abolitionist gathering just for them: the Anti-Slavery Convention of American Women. The organizers urged mothers to use their maternal influence to raise generations of abolitionists.

These women also saw their homemaking as vital work in the movement because it was in their homes, as in the Douglass and Garrison households, that critical anti-slavery work was conducted.

SARAH LOUISA FORTEN

Teenagers like soldiers Moore, Johnson, and Walters faced great danger and even death during the Civil War. Their military service was abolitionist work, because a Union victory meant the end of slavery.

Other Black abolitionist children and teenagers took part in anti-slavery work by writing, passing out movement pamphlets, and organizing anti-slavery associations made up of their peers. Sarah Forten, for example, was just seventeen years old when her poetry was featured in William Lloyd Garrison's *Liberator*. Her poem "The Grave of the Slave" recalls the despair and anguish a deceased enslaved man experienced in life. Forten contrasts the sorrow and cruelty of the slave's life with the power and control the white slave owner had over his life. The grave is a welcoming home for the unnamed enslaved person who experienced the harsh realities of bondage when he was alive:

> *The cold storms of winter shall chill him no more,*
> *His woes and his sorrows, his pains are all o'er;*
> *The sod of the valley now covers his form,*
> *He is safe in his last home, he feels not the storm.*

> *The poor slave is laid all unheeded and lone.*
> *Where the rich and the poor find a permanent home;*
> *Not his master can rouse him with voice of command;*
> *He knows not and hears not his cruel demand;*

> *Not a tear, nor a sigh to embalm his cold tomb,*
> *No friend to lament him, no child to bemoan;*
> *Not a stone marks the place where he peacefully lies,*
> *The earth for the pillow, his curtain the skies.*

Poor slave, shall we sorrow that death was thy friend,
The last and the kindest that heaven could send?
The grave of the weary is welcomed and blest;
And death to the captive is freedom and rest.

SARAH PARKER REMOND

The spark that ignited Sarah Parker Remond's work as an abolitionist was lit when she was just eight years old. Like most children, Sarah loved learning. But in the early 1800s education options for free Black children, even in the North, were scarce. After her parents worked to get Sarah and her two sisters enrolled in a local public school in Salem, Massachusetts, the eight-year-old was overjoyed!

The girls got along fine with the white students, and their white teachers welcomed them into their classrooms. However, some white parents didn't take too kindly to their children attending school with Black children, and Sarah and her sisters were forced to leave. The sadness and injustice Sarah felt changed her, and she would fight for women's rights and abolition for much of her life.

At age sixteen Remond began lecturing as an abolition speaker. As an adult, she was a featured

American Anti-Slavery Society speaker, and she traveled throughout the country. Eventually she began lecturing throughout Europe. In 1866 she joined the British suffragette movement and was one of the original fifteen hundred signers of the first petition for women's right to vote in Britian.

UNCLE TOM'S CABIN

Harriet Beecher Stowe was an American novelist whose groundbreaking slave narrative, *Uncle Tom's Cabin,* depicted the violence and immorality of slavery and was a rallying call to white Christians to demand the end of the practice in the United States. The novel uses melodrama—a creative writing style that exaggerates events, plots, and character personas—to show the depravity and brutality slave owners inflicted on their slaves.

Stowe was born in Litchfield, Connecticut, to parents Lyman Beecher and Roxana Foote Beecher. Her family was influential and of high social stature. Her father was a Congregational minister and president of Lane Seminary (a seminary is a school that trains ministers or rabbis). One of her brothers,

Henry Ward Beecher, was a famous preacher, religious reformer, and abolitionist who advocated for women's right to vote. To this day, he is revered by Christian and non-Christian social justice advocates alike.

A photograph of Harriet Beecher Stowe taken between 1854 and 1860.

Uncle Tom's Cabin brought Harriet her own notoriety as a writer and abolitionist.

Stowe wrote the novel after her son died of cholera, an infectious disease of the intestines. The loss of her son moved her to consider what enslaved Black women must've felt when their children were sold away from them. She was filled with emotions—grief and sorrow over her son's death, and sympathy for enslaved mothers who would never see their children again.

Stowe was a Christian, and she believed slavery was a sin. She hoped the novel would compel white Christian believers to take up abolitionist work. The novel tells the story of Uncle Tom, a loving and devout slave who saves the life of a little white girl named Eva.

Eva's father is so grateful that he purchases Uncle Tom, who becomes Eva's close friend and companion. But Eva is sickly, and as she gets sicker, she asks her father to free Uncle Tom when she dies. Although her father agrees, he is killed before he can free Uncle Tom.

Uncle Tom's new owner is the cruel and depraved Simon Legree, who enjoys turning his slaves into brutes who inflict pain on one another at his command. When Uncle Tom refuses to reveal the plans of escaped slaves, Legree has him whipped to death by Quimbo and Sambo, slaves who are forced to keep other slaves in line through violence and fear. Stowe uses dark imagery to describe the hellish trials and tribulations enslaved people endured. Her characters represent aspects of good and evil, sin and virtue, and the Christian god of the Bible and the devil.

After its publication in 1852, *Uncle Tom's Cabin* sold three hundred thousand copies in the first year alone. Abolitionists embraced the novel to further advocate for the end of slavery. Many pro-slavery advocates rejected the book outright, while some white writers used it as a prototype for writing pro-slavery melodramatic novels.

Today the novel is still taught in some middle and high schools, although it is frequently placed on banned books lists throughout the United States.

The term "Uncle Tom" has become a controversial racial slur that refers to a Black person who is docile and subservient to white people, someone who panders to white people's fantasies about happy Black slaves. Perhaps that's because Uncle Tom saves Eva and becomes her dutiful friend and companion before she dies. But Uncle Tom is also the novel's hero, who sacrifices his freedom and his life to save his fellow slaves.

THE FIRST NOVEL PUBLISHED BY AN AFRICAN AMERICAN WOMAN

In 1859, Harriet E. Wilson published *Our Nig; or, Sketches from the Life of a Free Black,* making her the first African American to publish a novel. Wilson was also the first Black woman to publish a book in English. Just as *Uncle Tom's Cabin* exposed Northern whites to the horrors of antebellum slavery, *Our Nig* was a shocking fictional account of the devastating impact racism and slavery had on free and enslaved Black people in the North. The book's title was controversial and offensive to some because of its reference to the racist and pejorative term "nigger," which has historically been used to demean and insult Black people. Wilson uses the term here to satirize—mock, criticize, ridicule—white Northerners who were supposedly against slavery, and uses irony to show that Black life in the North wasn't much better than it was in the South.

The book's protagonist is a biracial girl named Frado whose white mother abandons her to the care of the Bellmont family after the child's father dies. Frado is an indentured servant who suffers tremendous abuse and isolation in the white New England family's home. After years of cruelty at the hands of Mrs. Bellmont, Frado falls in love with Samuel, a runaway slave and abolitionist. But Frado's happiness is short-lived when Samuel abandons her and their child. Once again Frado is let down by the people she loves.

Although Frado is technically an indentured servant and not a slave, she has suffered more physical abuse than Samuel, who was once enslaved. Harriet Wilson uses irony in the novel to depict how Northern white people subjugated poor Black people, and how Northern states benefited from free Black labor while also criticizing Southern slavery.

Literary scholars of Wilson's life and novel argue that the writer uses the fictional Frado to depict the loss, emotional pain, and physical abuse she herself experienced as an indentured servant of a New

England family. Like Frado, Wilson was biracial, the daughter of a Black father and a poor white mother. Wilson's mother also abandoned her to a white family when her father died.

Through Frado, Wilson illustrates how Black indentured servants suffered in the North and how especially vulnerable free poor Black women were in free states.

SUSIE BAKER KING TAYLOR

Susie Baker King Taylor was born enslaved in Liberty County, Georgia, in 1848. Although born into slavery, she would grow up to lead a remarkable life of service, part of which included significant contributions to the Union Army's Thirty-Third U.S. Colored Infantry.

As a youngster, Susie Baker was raised on the Grest family plantation. The urban slavery traditions of Savannah, Georgia, allowed enslaved people to visit free relatives nearby and be hired out for work, and the Grests were unusually lenient because they allowed Susie and her brother to live with her free grandmother in Savannah. It was there that the seeds of service were planted by her grandmother, who made sure Susie learned to read and write. Because it was illegal for Black people to attend school and get an education, Susie's lessons were taught at a secret school for Black children. There would have been big trouble for her grandmother, the school's teachers, and Susie's classmates' parents if word had gotten out that Black children were being taught to read and write!

Susie quickly surpassed the other pupils and advanced beyond what the teachers could offer her. She was fortunate to have as a playmate her landlord's son, who encouraged her love of learning. By the time she was fourteen years old, she was secretly teaching other Black children and their parents too without arousing the suspicion of local white people. Because she could write, Susie also created fake travel passes for free and enslaved Black people so they could travel freely at night without fear of arrest by white patrolmen. She was doing dangerous abolition work!

In 1862, Susie fled to the Union Army line around Savannah to seek refuge, because although she lived with her free grandmother, she herself was still enslaved. But Susie was not alone; by the time she arrived, thousands of other fugitive slaves had sought and found refuge with the Union Army. They were considered "contraband" by the U.S. Army—enslaved people who had escaped to or volunteered to help the Union Army.

The Union Army transported Susie and the other runaways to a contraband camp on Saint Simons Island, off the coast of Georgia. Early on, Susie stood out among the other refugees. When Union soldiers learned she could read and write, they enlisted her to teach the many contraband children, and their parents as well. At the young age of

Susie Baker King Taylor, known as the first African American army nurse.

fourteen Susie Baker started the first school run by a Black woman to educate free Black children!

Susie Baker worked as a nurse, cook, laundry worker, and teacher in the First South Carolina Volunteers, the first Black regiment to support the Union Army during the Civil War. After the war she returned to Savannah and made several attempts at leading her own school but failed due to competition with newly established public schools for free Black children. Unable to find work as a teacher, she took the only work most Black women could find: as domestic help.

When the family she worked for moved to Boston, Massachusetts, in 1874, Susie accompanied them. She was amazed by the relative degree of acceptance Black people experienced there. She threw her support behind Black veterans and helped establish Corps Sixty-Seven of the Women's Relief Corps, a volunteer charity that raised money to support Black veterans.

In 1902 she published *Reminiscences of My Life in Camp with the 33d United States Colored Troops, Late 1st S. C. Volunteers.* It is the only memoir written by a Black woman documenting what life was like working alongside the Thirty-Third U.S. Colored Infantry during the Civil War. In the book she writes: "They say, 'One flag, one nation, one country indivisible.' Is this true? Can we say this truthfully, when one race is allowed to burn, hang, and inflict the most horrible torture weekly, monthly, on another? No, we cannot sing 'My country, 'tis of thee, Sweet land of Liberty'! It is hollow mockery."

LET'S THINK ABOUT THIS

1. Why were white people threatened by the idea of Black people learning to read?

2. How did literacy help Black people argue the need for abolition and the emancipation of those enslaved?

3. Why was Harriet Beecher Stowe's novel such an effective weapon in the abolition movement?

4. Why did Harriet Wilson choose to create a work of fiction rather than write her autobiography?

CHAPTER 5

RECONSTRUCTION

Once it was apparent that the Union Army was headed for a clear victory over the Confederates and the abolition of slavery would become a reality, Lincoln turned his attention to unification of the country. He envisioned a way forward that guaranteed the uncontested freedom of newly emancipated Blacks in the South and was very beneficial to Confederate loyalists, who could've been charged with treason and tried in court for their part in the secession of the Southern states.

Lincoln's proposed Proclamation of Amnesty and Reconstruction would essentially absolve Confederate slaveholders and soldiers for any part they had played in the war against the Union. Lincoln saw this as a way to restore goodwill among white men when the Southern states were readmitted to the United States. It would pardon former Confederate soldiers for treason against the country and even pay former slave and plantation owners restitution, a financial equivalent for land and property—excluding chattel slaves—that had been damaged or destroyed in the war.

If you're thinking the Confederate states would get off easy under this plan, you are right! All they had to do in exchange for such leniency was pledge their allegiance to the United States and recognize emancipation as law.

Believe it or not, there were still many who refused to agree to Lincoln's terms. Most Southern whites remained bitter over the defeat and the end of slavery. For Southern plantation owners the loss of slaves meant the loss of free labor, which had fueled their agricultural business, and they just couldn't get over the federal government interfering with their livelihoods and Southern way of life.

Their refusal of amnesty didn't stop Lincoln's Amnesty and Reconstruction plan because it required only 10 percent of a state's population to accept the terms and conditions of the plan and swear their allegiance to the Union. That allowed Confederate states to be readmitted to the Union even if the majority of their citizens didn't pledge allegiance to the United States or honor emancipation.

While Lincoln was looking forward, many Southern whites still held on to the past and resented being forced into a new way of life free of slavery.

Throughout Reconstruction, which lasted from 1865 to 1877, the newly reunified nation was divided along political and racial lines, similar to those that had sparked the Civil War in the first place.

Ironically, while Lincoln earned the nickname of the "Great Emancipator" for his success in freeing the slaves, his Amnesty and Reconstruction plan paid little attention to the needs of the 4 million newly freed African Americans who had few to no resources when the war ended.

Members of Lincoln's own Republican Party thought his plan for Amnesty and Reconstruction let the former Confederate leaders and their constituents (the people they represented) off too easily. They believed allowing Confederate states to rejoin with only 10 percent of the population's sworn oath to the United States was problematic. The plan was much too easy on Southern states because it allowed their readmittance to the nation, paid them for economic losses they had due to the war, and required very few concessions in exchange.

So Republicans rejected Lincoln's Amnesty and Reconstruction plan, and Congress passed the Wade-Davis Bill instead. This new plan included harsh penalties for the former Confederate states, ensured civil rights for Black people, and required a majority of a state's voters (at that time only white men) to pledge their oath to the United States as conditions. It restricted Confederate leaders from holding public office as well as listing other state-level requirements. Republicans didn't want to give the former Confederate states an easy pass, and just as important, they wanted to make sure African Americans were recognized as citizens and had protections under the law.

But President Lincoln vetoed the bill, which went much further than his original Amnesty and Reconstruction plan, and it never became law.

Reconstruction was a time of political ping-pong. Republicans would establish programs and initiatives to help the newly freed African Americans. Democrats, who grew to include former Confederate leaders and sympathizers, ran for political office and, after winning, blocked measures to help African Americans, created laws to marginalize them, and established policies that supported a white supremacist society.

For example, even before the war was over, Union general William Tecumseh Sherman issued Special Field Order 15, approved by Lincoln, which would provide formerly enslaved people with forty acres of coastal Georgia, Florida, and South Carolina land on which to settle and farm. They had been farming for white plantation owners for several generations; owning their land meant they could now benefit from the harvests they reaped.

The idea for land redistribution to African Americans came from Black leaders who had a meeting with General Sherman. Sherman wanted to find out what the newly freed slaves needed. Those present answered that they needed land to build communities apart from white people, whom they distrusted and believed would do them harm. They also understood land ownership as wealth and a means for their people to accumulate more of it. General Sherman had a similar idea because his order stated that the newly formed all-Black communities would be self-governed and set apart from the rest of the nation.

Later on, General Sherman also threw in a mule, which the U.S. government would lend to new landowners, who would need the working animal to help them farm their land.

We know that roughly forty thousand African Americans received "forty acres and a mule"—out of the 4 million newly freed. To add to the injustice, Lincoln's assassination signaled the death of the "forty acres and a mule" initiative when President Andrew Johnson not only put a stop to the agreement but also seized land that had been given to free Blacks and returned it to the original Confederate landowners.

Economists estimate that forty acres and a mule for each formerly enslaved person would have cost the United States $640 billion in today's dollars.

THE FREEDMEN'S BUREAU

In March 1865, just before the end of the Civil War, the Bureau of Refugees, Freedmen, and Abandoned Lands, known as the Freedmen's Bureau, was set up to temporarily help the millions of newly freed slaves who had few financial resources. Freedmen had to figure out how to feed themselves and their families, since they were no longer living on plantations and didn't have jobs. Recognizing the challenges the 4 million newly emancipated men, women, and children were facing, Congress established the Freedmen's Bureau to provide food, medical attention, legal help, and lodging for newly freed African Americans who had nowhere to go and no means of employment.

The bureau operated in the former Confederate states and the border states. With roughly nine hundred staff members, the federal agency served millions of freedmen and established hospitals, schools, and what are today called historically Black colleges and universities, or HBCUs, including Howard University in Washington, D.C., Nashville's Fisk University, and the Hampton Normal and Agricultural Institute in Hampton, Virginia. Bureau staff also helped freedmen find lost loved ones, secured resources for veterans, and settled labor disputes with white employers.

Their work wasn't easy, because they faced opposition and violence from Southern whites who resented the help they offered Black people. Like the newly freed Blacks, bureau staff experienced threats and intimidation from angry white individuals and the Ku Klux Klan.

The work of bureau staff led to improvements to Southern Black people's lives. But in 1872 all offices were dismantled due to objections from Southern whites who were angry about the government's help for freedmen.

The end of slavery brought exhilaration and happiness, along with uncertainty about the future.

A racist ad attacking the Freedman's Bureau, advocating the election of Hiester Clymer, who ran for Pennsylvania governor (and lost) on a white-supremacy platform in 1866.

SCHOOLS FOR FREE BLACKS

Education was a top priority for newly freed African Americans. Before the Civil War only 15 percent of African Americans were literate. During Reconstruction, the Freedmen's Bureau provided funds to establish public and private schools to educate free Blacks. Some of the new schools were also financially supported by religious associations like the American Missionary Association.

One such school was the Avery Normal Institute,

established in 1865. Avery was a private school and the first accredited secondary school for African American students in Charleston, South Carolina. At Avery boys and girls were taught science, theater arts, philosophy, and foreign languages, which was on par with the education white males received at that time.

The Avery Institute was the training ground for African Americans who went on to become college-educated teachers, artists, architects, and political leaders in South Carolina and throughout the country. Today the Avery building houses the College of Charleston's Avery Research Center for African American History and Culture, which holds a repository for archival materials and special collections, an art gallery, and a programming space open to students, faculty, and the general public.

The Freedmen's Bureau also partnered with religious organizations to open three thousand schools for Black children during Reconstruction. Many graduates returned to their former schools to teach the next generations of students.

But teaching Black students wasn't always a safe job, because Southern whites still opposed Blacks' learning to read and write. They believed educated Black people would no longer "know their place" as the inferior race, so they did what they could to interfere with their learning. Their tactics included intimidation, violence, and destruction of Black schools to keep Black students from learning.

PRESIDENT JOHNSON'S VISION FOR RECONSTRUCTION

After Lincoln's assassination, Vice President Andrew Johnson took office as president of the United States. Unlike Lincoln, he wasn't an abolitionist. In fact he was a proud slave owner who boasted that he owned slaves.

To say Johnson was a complicated presidential successor is an understatement. Johnson was a Southerner from Tennessee who had not supported secession. He sided and fought with the Union to maintain the country, but not because he was anti-slavery. At one point as Lincoln's vice president, he lobbied the president to exempt his home state of Tennessee from the Emancipation Proclamation!

So it shouldn't be much of a surprise that when he rose to the seat of American power, President Johnson unveiled and enacted his own presidential Reconstruction plan, one that was very different from the one Lincoln had had in mind.

Johnson's plan stipulated that states ratify—or agree to the legally binding specifics of—the Thirteenth Amendment and required all white Southern landowners to petition him directly for the return of their land—including the land that had been given to freedmen as part of Special Field Order 15. Johnson felt no allegiance to the formerly enslaved, so he sided with the white people (former Confederates) who petitioned him to get their land back. By doing so, Johnson made it impossible for African Americans to retain their new lands, and thus their chances for attaining wealth and stability.

Eventually President Johnson sided completely with Southern whites and decreed that all land given to freedmen in accordance with Special Field Order 15 must be returned to white ownership. Increasingly, Johnson openly embraced white supremacy, stating, "White men alone must manage the South."

Southern whites seized on Johnson's leniency toward them as an opportunity to elect former Confederates who had not been charged for their roles in the secession to state and federal roles. Once they were in power again, leaders of Southern states began to enact laws to stifle freedmen living within their states. They created laws known as "Black Codes" that limited African Americans' ability to work and live freely with the rights due to all American citizens. The Black Codes were one form of white backlash African Americans experienced throughout Reconstruction and well into the twentieth century.

Freedmen found themselves experiencing a new form of slavery, one without actual chains. Black Codes limited the kind of work African Americans could do to domestic work and sharecropping—the same tasks they had done while enslaved—with very little pay.

Black Codes also made it legal to arrest Black men who were unemployed and force them into servitude in chain gangs, where Black men were literally chained together while doing such things as working in quarries or building railroads. If a white man needed extra help, he could pay the bail bond of Black men who had been arrested for "loitering," which is walking or standing in public. Once that white man paid the bail bond, the Black man had to work off the payment for any length of time the white man stipulated. Some Black men had to work years to pay off bonds as little as a couple of hundred dollars!

Southern whites had found a way to re-enslave free African Americans.

THE FOURTEENTH AND FIFTEENTH AMENDMENTS

Republicans continued to advocate for the newly freed population, pushing for federal measures to ensure their constitutional rights. They used their power to pass legislation that would protect African Americans—most important, the Fourteenth and Fifteenth Amendments to the United States Constitution.

Abolitionists, Republicans, and suffrage activists believed passage of the Fourteenth and Fifteenth Amendments would ensure African Americans' constitutional protections and full enfranchisement (the right to vote), and they would be free to exercise the rights of all American citizens. The Fourteenth Amendment was passed by Congress on June 13, 1866, and ratified July 9, 1868. It granted citizenship to everyone born in the United States. Passage of the Fourteenth Amendment was a major victory for African Americans because it granted them citizenship, the right to a fair trial by their peers in criminal cases, and full protection under the law.

The Fifteenth Amendment was passed by Congress February 26, 1869, and ratified February 3, 1870. It granted all men the right to vote regardless of race, color, or prior enslavement.

But not Black women. It's true. Black women and white women alike could not cast their own votes in political elections. Both groups had worked alongside Black and white abolitionist men to force the U.S. government to end slavery before the Civil War, and they also worked collectively on suffrage, or the right to vote. Without this right, they could not fully effect political change on the local and national levels.

BLACK VOTING RIGHTS ACTIVISTS

African American abolitionists and thought leaders, including Frederick Douglass, Sojourner Truth, Ida B. Wells, and Frances Ellen Watkins Harper worked alongside white suffragettes such as Lucretia Mott, Elizabeth Cady Stanton, and Susan B. Anthony to secure voting rights for African Americans and women.

Sojourner Truth, born Isabella Baumfree, was an abolitionist, suffragette, preacher, and proponent of the temperance movement, a socio-religious movement that advocated for complete abstinence from alcohol and for moderation in all worldly pleasures. Truth was born into slavery in Ulster County, in upstate New York. Like most enslaved people, she experienced brutal physical violence and heartbreak at the hands of enslavers. Truth was sold several times

I SELL THE SHADOW TO SUPPORT THE SUBSTANCE.
SOJOURNER TRUTH.

An 1864 portrait of Sojourner Truth. The quote at the bottom reads: "I sell the shadow to support the substance."

throughout her time in enslavement, but in 1827 a local abolitionist family helped her by purchasing her freedom, and Truth escaped slavery with her youngest child. Truth's abolitionist friends also helped her file suit for the return of Peter, one of her other children, who had been illegally sold to Alabama slave owners. Both luck and the law were on her side, because in the state of New York, it was illegal to sell any enslaved person out of the state and all minors were guaranteed freedom at age twenty-one.

Truth's personal experiences shaped her views on abolition and women's rights. She was an associate of Frederick Douglass and William Lloyd Garrison and was such an influential abolitionist leader that President Abraham Lincoln invited her to the White House for a meeting. Truth toured the nation preaching and advocating for rights for women and African Americans.

Sojourner Truth's courage was colossal; while traveling to meet President Lincoln in Washington, D.C., she defiantly traveled in whites-only streetcars, well over a century before civil rights activist Rosa Parks refused to give up her seat in the whites-only section of a Birmingham bus.

Truth is known to most people for giving the "Ain't I a Woman?" speech. While it is true that she gave an emotionally charged and radical speech advocating for Black women's rights at the 1851 Ohio Women's Rights Convention, the repeated rhetorical question wasn't a part of her comments. Over the years writers took some creative license when recounting her speech, most likely to make her sound more like a slave born and raised in the South.

But Truth never lived in the South, and for most of her childhood she spoke only Dutch, so it is unlikely that she suddenly started speaking like Southern slaves much later in her life.

Another important activist was Ida B. Wells, born enslaved in 1862 in Holly Springs, Mississippi. After slavery ended, her parents became political activists during the Reconstruction era. Like her parents, Wells advocated for African American rights and protections under the law. A gifted writer, journalist, and speaker, Wells exposed lynchings and mob violence against African Americans in the late nineteenth and early twentieth centuries.

Frances Ellen Watkins Harper was a writer, poet, lecturer, abolitionist, and suffragist. She was also the first African American woman to publish a short story. Harper believed Black women were subjugated because of their race as well as their gender. That was why she was so passionate about suffrage for Black women.

Many of the white women fighting for voting rights had also been abolitionists and had used their voices and influence to advocate for abolition. However, when Black men got the right to vote before them, white suffragettes—women seeking the right to vote—were angered and frustrated. Dismayed by the Fifteenth Amendment, Black and white women alike remained steadfast in their goal of attaining women's suffrage. They were determined to get the right to vote!

Black women also continued to fight for civil rights for themselves and Black men. White women were the face of the suffragette effort, although Black women were actively engaged in efforts to gain the right to vote. When American women got the right to vote with the passage of the Nineteenth Amendment, they did what they had accused Black men of doing when they gained the right to vote with the

Fifteenth Amendment: they forgot about the Black women who had been fighting alongside them the whole time.

FROM SLAVERY TO POLITICAL LEADERSHIP

If you attend a public school in the United States, you have Robert Smalls and Joseph Hayne Rainey, two Black South Carolina politicians, to thank for it. In 1868, just three years after the Civil War ended, Smalls and Rainey were the masterminds behind public education.

Smalls was born in Beaufort, South Carolina, where he and his mother, Lydia Polite, lived as enslaved people owned by Henry McKee, a white planter. Although the identity of his father is unknown, we do know that he was a white man, possibly McKee or his son, John. Smalls and his mother lived in small slave quarters behind McKee's house at 511 Prince Street in Beaufort, where his mother was a house slave. As a youngster, Smalls was not allowed to attend school, and when he was twelve years old, McKee hired him out as a waiter and dockhand miles away in Charleston Harbor. Although Smalls was actually doing the work, McKee got to keep the wages he made.

In Charleston, Smalls met the love of his life. Hannah Jones was also enslaved, and although marriages between slaves were not recognized in the eyes of the law, the young couple married anyway in 1856. Their hopes for wedded bliss were cut short when the Civil War began in 1861 and Smalls was sent to work as a crewmember on the *Planter,* a maritime vessel used by the Confederate Army.

Early in the war Confederate soldiers racked up numerous victories against the Union Army. The city of Charleston was heavily protected by massive fortifications at Fort Moultrie and Fort Sumter, making it virtually impenetrable. Fear seized Smalls as he saw this advantage and recognized that a Confederate victory would mean no hope of freedom for him, his family, or millions of enslaved people throughout the South.

So he devised a daring plan! At only twenty-three years old, Smalls concocted a plot to steal the *Planter* and sail right past unsuspecting Confederate soldiers at Fort Sumter and Fort Moultrie.

When the white crew members went into Charleston for drinks and entertainment, leaving the vessel in the hands of the enslaved Black men, Smalls and the others sprang into action. Once they set sail, they picked up their families, who were ashore nearby awaiting their arrival. After rescuing their loved ones, the freedom seekers sailed for open waters. They weren't in the clear just yet; their freedom depended on getting past heavily armed Confederate battalions at the forts.

But Smalls had planned for that too! He wore a captain's hat as a disguise as he piloted the steamer, and when they came near Confederate forces, he used the proper maritime signals used by the Confederate Navy. The Confederate Navy had its own maritime signals to communicate between its vessels, which Smalls had learned working on the *Planter*. Confederate naval officers were none the wiser, and Smalls and the rest of the fugitives aboard the *Planter* sailed straight into Union waters, right into freedom.

As a free man, Robert Smalls spent the rest of his life working for the public good as a Union naval pilot, a businessman, and a visionary in state and national politics.

Joseph H. Rainey had an equally impressive political career as the first African American elected to the U.S. House of Representatives in 1870. Like Smalls, Rainey had been born into slavery in South Carolina. Both of his parents were enslaved by plantation owners in the Lowcountry town of Georgetown, a seaside town noted for rice cultivation, one of the most lucrative slave enterprises of the time. As was customary with some slave owners, Rainey's father was allowed to keep a portion of the wages he earned working as a barber for local white men. Eventually his father earned enough money to buy his family's freedom.

Although they were free, they had very few opportunities for employment. Since South Carolina prohibited Black children, both enslaved and free, to obtain an education, Rainey never attended school as a child. Instead, he became a barber like his father. In Charleston Rainey was a popular barber at the upscale Mills Hotel (which still exists today in the same location on Meeting Street). Rainey met his wife while visiting Philadelphia in 1859, and the young couple returned to Charleston, where they settled down.

Little did they know the Civil War would break out just two years later. Joseph Rainey found himself in an unthinkable predicament when Confederate soldiers used violence and intimidation to force him and other Black men to build forts and other physical barriers for defense against the Union Army.

Like Smalls, Rainey knew he had to do something. In 1862 Rainey and his family made their escape to Bermuda, which had abolished slavery some thirty years before. The Raineys stowed away on a blockade runner, a fast merchant vessel used to slip through military blockades. On the island the Raineys became wealthy business owners.

They didn't return to the United States until the Civil War had ended.

Rainey's political career began when the Republican Party nominated him for a South Carolina seat in the U.S. House of Representatives upon the resignation of Representative Benjamin Franklin Whittemore in 1870 due to accusations of political misconduct. Rainey served the rest of Whittemore's term (1869–1871) and then was elected to the full 1871–1873 term. In both electoral races, Rainey's political rival, C. W. Dudley, was not only a member of the rival Democratic Party, he was also a white man. Yet South Carolina voters—the majority of whom were white men—did not let race stop them from electing Joseph H. Rainey to represent them in Congress for two terms!

Smalls and Rainey were forward-thinking politicians who believed in equity and justice for all Americans. Having lived as enslaved people, they knew firsthand the suffering and injustices Black South Carolinians had endured and continued to endure even after the war had ended. Their experiences fueled their resolve to help their people and all South Carolinians, regardless of race.

Together, Smalls and Rainey introduced state laws to make sure all South Carolina children had access to public education. Their radical vision—that all children should have the opportunity to learn and to become literate—was written into the South Carolina state constitution at the 1868 state convention. It was the first legislation of its kind anywhere and it paved the way for federal, state, and local legislation throughout the country, making public education accessible to American children in the South, North, and burgeoning West. Smalls and Rainey were innovative political thinkers whose contributions to American education are still relevant today.

South Carolina legislators Robert Smalls and Joseph Hayne Rainey.

BRIEF POLITICAL PROGRESS

During Reconstruction, newly freed African Americans and those who had secured their freedom before the Civil War took full advantage of their new rights as American citizens, including the right to hold public office if elected.

In 1870, the same year Joseph H. Rainey was elected to the U.S. House of Representatives, Hiram Rhodes Revels was the first African American elected to the U.S. Senate. Revels was born free in Fayetteville, North Carolina. Like his father, Revels was a minister who preached to free and enslaved African Americans before the Civil War. During the war he served as a chaplain to African American Union soldiers.

Revels began his political career when he was elected alderman for the town of Natchez, Mississippi, before being elected to the Mississippi state legislature. In 1870 he was elected to represent Mississippi in the United States Senate, assuming the seat that had been vacated by Democrat Albert Brown, who left when Mississippi seceded the nation. A total of sixteen African Americans were elected to Congress during Reconstruction, and nearly two thousand African Americans were elected to local, state, and federal government roles. In 2024, there were fifty-nine African Americans in the House of Representatives and four U.S. senators.

As African Americans gained political influence, Southern white politicians enacted legal barriers and obstacles to stop African American progress. Many of those measures would continue to negatively affect African Americans throughout the next century.

• • •

Granville T. Woods

If you've been to an amusement park, there's a chance you have seen and even mustered up the nerve to ride a high-speed, heart-dropping roller coaster like Six Flags' Superman, which features a two-hundred-foot drop. A nineteenth-century African American inventor developed the prototype for that ride in 1892 with his Figure Eight roller coaster at Brooklyn's Coney Island.

Some have dubbed Granville T. Woods the "Black Edison" because his inventions, produced around the same time as Thomas Edison's, were so revolutionary.

Woods was born free in Columbus, Ohio, in 1856. As a teenager, he worked a number of jobs that ignited his curiosity about engineering and gave him valuable on-the-job experience, including as an actual railroad engineer. Like most Black people back then, Woods didn't receive much formal education as a youngster, but as an adult he was able to take classes in engineering and electricity while living in New York for a short time. You could say these experiences sparked Woods's joy in using science to find solutions for improving everyday life.

Woods was responsible for some of the most important inventions of the nineteenth century, such as the induction telegraph, which allows train conductors to speak to one another over telegraph wires, and the telephone transmitter.

The induction telegraph increased passenger safety, because train conductors could transmit important information to prevent train collisions. Woods's telephone transmitter combined the telephone and telegraph, creating an improved voice transmission system. Alexander Graham Bell is known as the inventor of the modern telephone in 1876, but years later he purchased Woods's patent for a new and improved telephone transmitter. With the money from the sale of his patent, Woods devoted his time to developing many other inventions that revolutionized life for people in the United States and around the world.

When he died in 1910, Woods had invented fifteen appliances and owned sixty patents for inventions that would be used to manufacture appliances still used today.

• • •

WHITE BACKLASH

For over two hundred years before Lincoln signed his wartime decree to end slavery, enslaved Black people had hoped for their liberation. But when their emancipation actually happened, it looked and felt very different from their long-held dreams of being free. That's because Southern whites resented the fact that they no longer had the legal right to force Black people to work without pay.

They now shunned the people they had forcibly brought to the South in chains. And, in their wrath, Southern whites did whatever they could to instill fear into freedmen and keep them from gaining wealth. They quickly began strategizing ways to marginalize and discriminate against the millions of newly emancipated people. If they couldn't own Black people, they would do everything in their power to keep them from experiencing full citizenship in this new American era.

In many ways, Lincoln's grand vision of a new South backfired. With amnesty for their war crimes, Confederate loyalists took all the benefits Lincoln's plan offered and gave nothing in exchange. The death and destruction of the Civil War hadn't changed their minds about slavery and states' rights to self-govern without interference from the federal government.

They set about doing all they could to ensure white Southern culture was preserved. Their political tactics included legal obstacles to keep African American men from voting, such as literacy tests and grandfather clauses, which stipulated that only those citizens whose grandfathers had been eligible to vote could themselves vote. They instituted legal barriers to prosperity, education, and overall quality of life.

Southern whites also used violence and intimidation to scare African Americans and keep them in their place. They established local militias (volunteer armed forces) to police Black people and limited where they could go and live. These security forces routinely terrorized Black families and entire communities, and when white mobs vandalized their homes, schools, and businesses, members of the militia were right there, taking part in the violence and mayhem.

As a result, Black people lived in constant fear. They had no protection. Life lived as free people felt like life in bondage in some ways.

LYNCHINGS AND MASSACRES

Between 1865 and 1877 some two thousand African Americans were lynched, or hanged to death, by white people in the United States. By the mid-twentieth century that number would double. White people used lynching to strike fear into African Americans throughout the South. Many lynchings were public spectacles, with white families—including children—in attendance. These brutal murders were not treated as crimes, and relatives of lynching victims did not see justice for their losses.

Sometimes the lynchers shot, burned, and cut off the limbs and genitals of Black victims before they hanged them from trees for everyone in the community to see. Lynchings were a form of white backlash that would continue well into the next century.

Most lynchings occurred when a Black person—typically a man—was accused of a crime like the murder or rape of a white woman, almost always without any evidence at all. After being "convicted"—trials were often rushed, with white jurors who harbored racist beliefs about Black people—the "guilty" individual would be carted off by an angry mob that would carry out the torture and lynching. It wasn't unusual for law-enforcement agents to take part in the ghoulish acts.

When lynch mobs dismembered their victims, they gave away body parts as souvenirs to onlookers who took pleasure in the ghastly spectacle.

Today there is a movement to commemorate the victims of these gruesome crimes that African Americans endured. The Legacy Museum, the National Memorial for Peace and Justice, and Freedom Monument Sculpture Park, all in Montgomery, Alabama, were developed by the Equal Justice Initiative to document and preserve African American lived experiences, even the most painful ones like lynching.

The Legacy Museum is an interactive space that traces Black life from the transatlantic slave trade through American history. The National Memorial for Peace and Justice documents every Black lynching in the historic record and honors the lives lost. Freedom Monument Sculpture Park features lifelike stone creations that offer an immersive examination of African American history on seventeen acres of land along the Alabama River.

Together these cultural sites further our understanding of American chattel slavery and what enslaved Africans and African Americans endured, as well as what they contributed to this country.

AMERICAN POLICING IS ROOTED IN SLAVERY

Did you know that modern American law enforcement can be traced back to slavery? Well, it's true. The earliest organized American "policing" began as slave patrols in the early 1700s. As the slave population grew in the Carolinas, the colonists were afraid slaves might lead insurrections, break free from bondage, or worse, repay them with the same violence they had used to control generations of enslaved Black people. Throughout slavery and the post-slavery Reconstruction era, the foundation of what we now see in city, county, state, and federal police agencies was taking shape to keep the growing slave population and, subsequently, free Blacks in line.

In the early days of slavery, wealthy plantation owners paid ruthless men to patrol the area and maintain the compliance of enslaved people through brute force and violent tactics. Slave patrols used fear to control the slave population by making examples of unruly slaves through torture and intimidation. Hiring slave-catching bounty hunters became popular as more and more enslaved people escaped bondage and fled to free states. Slave catchers were unscrupulous trackers who used lies and tricks to entrap fugitive slaves they were paid to find, along with other runaways and even free Blacks whom they then illegally sold into slavery!

When slavery was over, slave patrols and slave catchers evolved once again. This time, white men formed local militias that policed the newly freed Black population. During Reconstruction, the Ku Klux Klan (KKK) became the most infamous white supremacist organization in the United States. KKK history dates back to 1865, when Confederate veterans began gathering as a private association to devise ways to control the Black population.

While Lincoln believed the Proclamation of Amnesty and Reconstruction would turn the page on the Confederacy, the very opposite was true. In fact, many Southern whites remained loyal to the defeated Confederacy and held out hope for a return of the "peculiar institution" of slavery. Their desire to return to antebellum life led them to devise tactics to control the newly freed Black population.

The origins of police departments and law-enforcement agencies across the nation are found in the slave patrols and local militias that were empowered to control enslaved and free Black people. This means they also share a foundational history of white supremacy, and of violence toward and intimidation of Black people. Some social justice activists see the high statistics of police brutality against Black people and the killings of Black suspects at the hands of police as being directly related to law enforcement's roots in slavery. They believe it is impossible for law enforcers to view Black people objectively when it comes to crime and policing because the institutions were created to control Black people from the very beginning.

That is why some activists have called for the defunding of the police. They believe American police and other law-enforcement entities are naturally biased to think of Black people as violent criminals who can be controlled only by intimidation and fear—because that was their mission in the first place.

PLESSY V. FERGUSON

The case of *Plessy v. Ferguson* was a daring legal experiment to challenge rampant discrimination against Black people and guarantee their civil liberties.

Homer Adolph Plessy was an African American man (he was actually seven-eighths white, but during slavery and Reconstruction anyone with "one drop" of Black blood was considered Black) who was enlisted by lawyers to challenge segregated seating on East Louisiana Railroad passenger trains. When Plessy refused to move from the "whites only" seating area, he was arrested. Plessy's attorneys filed suit and argued that segregated seating violated the Thirteenth Amendment (which ended slavery) and the Fourteenth Amendment (which guaranteed the formerly enslaved their civil rights).

But the white Supreme Court justices didn't see it that way. Instead, they ruled that states had the right to enforce segregation between the races. The *Plessy* ruling is an example of how whites used the judicial system to control Black people.

Plessy's loss meant Black people were not actually American citizens and were not entitled to the rights outlined in the Bill of Rights. With the stroke of a pen, the Supreme Court justices rolled back the Reconstruction protections Blacks had gained with the Civil Rights Act of 1875, which guaranteed "the full and equal enjoyment of any of the accommodations, advantages, facilities, and privileges of inns, public conveyances on land or water, theaters and other places of public amusement; subject only to the conditions and limitations established by law, and applicable alike to citizens of every race and color."

Without protections under the law, free Black people were just as vulnerable as they were during slavery.

The *Plessy* ruling and Jim Crow laws were used like Black Codes of the past—to maintain a society built on white supremacy—and African Americans once again had no rights. Southern white men who were angered by gains made by free Blacks after slavery saw their Supreme Court victory as bringing them one step closer to a return to antebellum years, when slavery was the customary and legal way of life in the South.

Black Codes and Jim Crow laws had the same goal, to subjugate and control Black people, but existed at different times. Black Codes were established right after slavery was abolished. Jim Crow laws were created to strip Black people of new rights gained with the passage of the Fourteenth Amendment and the Fifteenth Amendment (which gave Black men the right to vote). Jim Crow laws also legalized segregation, which made it illegal for Blacks and whites to sit, eat, work, or walk alongside one another. They couldn't drink from the same water fountains. Black and white children couldn't play with one another, and they attended separate "whites only" and "colored only" schools.

Blacks and whites who fell in love were legally prohibited from getting married. A Black person who violated this law or was suspected of doing so faced jail, violent beatings, and even death in many instances. It would be a whole century before the United States Supreme Court would rule that the marriage of Mildred Loving, a Black woman, to Richard Loving, a white man, was legal under the law. The 1967 Virginia Supreme Court ruling determined that interracial couples who wanted to marry were protected by the Fourteenth Amendment. That meant any state laws that prohibited interracial marriage were in violation of that Civil Rights Act.

Jim Crow laws were used to discriminate against African Americans and keep them second-class citizens. Things wouldn't change for Blacks until the middle of the twentieth century, when they secured significant civil rights with *Brown v. Board of Education of Topeka* in 1954, which mandated the desegregation of public schools, and the passage of the 1964 Civil Rights Act, which guaranteed Black people's right to vote and other protections as citizens. The twentieth-century fight for Black liberation would focus on desegregation of schools and public places and securing the right to vote for all citizens. It would be violent, and many Black men, women, and children and white allies would lose their lives standing up against injustices.

The push for Black civil rights would be led by grassroots leaders from different parts of the country. Some were old, but many were young adults and college students. They held many different ideas about what Black liberation looked like and what they should do to win it. Some were radicals in the tradition of John Brown, and others were nonviolent like the pacifist Quakers. Black women played major roles throughout the different movements, yet Black men held the spotlight as courageous leaders and gifted orators, just as Frederick Douglass had during the previous century.

The achievements of the twentieth-century Civil Rights Movement wouldn't just secure rights for African Americans; they paved the way for immigrants, women, and LGBTQ+ Americans to fight for and win rights and protections as American citizens.

LET'S THINK ABOUT THIS

1. How different might life have been for newly freed African Americans and their descendants if they had all received forty acres of land and a mule?

2. Why did journalists want Sojourner Truth to sound like she was from the South when they reprinted accounts of her speech?

3. How did the efforts of activists like Sojourner Truth, Ida B. Wells, and Frances Ellen Watkins Harper contribute to the fight for civil rights, and what can we learn from their activism today?

POLITICAL PROGRESSION AND REGRESSION

Barack Hussein Obama was the forty-fourth president of the United States and the first Black president in the country's history. With his inauguration on January 20, 2009, the Obamas became the first Black presidential family to ever live in the White House. President Obama, First Lady Michelle Obama, and daughters Malia and Sasha lived for eight years in the nation's most iconic home, which had been built with slave labor.

President Obama's historic election as the nation's commander in chief was a grassroots effort that welcomed people from all walks of life to join together to make the country live up to its founding precepts that all men are created equal, that they are endowed by their Creator with certain unalienable Rights, that among these are Life, Liberty and the pursuit of Happiness, as written in the Declaration of Independence. Using the motto "Yes We Can," the Obama campaign embraced diversity and inclusion as tools for unifying voters, and the country by extension.

For many Black people, Obama's election was a hope and dream they had never thought was possible.

Some Americans felt his election to the country's seat of power, making him the leader of the free world, meant racism was dead in the United States. They started speaking of a post-racial society. Barack Obama's historic election had to mean that change had finally come.

But in some ways the total opposite was true. Political differences divided the country even further. For the first time in American history, some media political commentators and analysts used racist stereotypes to describe the sitting president. The Tea (Taxed Enough Already) Party emerged as a burgeoning unofficial third political party founded on conservative principles, with some of its leaders responsible for promoting the false "birther" claim that Obama wasn't born in the United States. Many racists flocked to the new party because it was an organized way to denounce the Obama presidency.

The Tea Party and increasing white supremacist opposition to President Obama were twenty-first-century forms of white backlash to Black progress, just like the backlash seen during Reconstruction.

Americans grew even more divided on issues of race with the 2012 murder of teenager Trayvon Martin by George Zimmerman, a white man who racially profiled and assaulted the unarmed teen before fatally shooting him. Using Florida's "stand your ground" law, which gives citizens the right to shoot a suspect if they merely feel they are being threatened,

President Barack Obama taking the oath of office at his first inauguration in 2009, with Michelle Obama by his side.

Zimmerman was acquitted of all charges. African Americans were stunned by the verdict, and Black parents worried about their children's safety. In the subsequent years of the Obama presidency, shooting deaths of unarmed Black people continued to make headline news.

On August 9, 2014, Ferguson, Missouri, police officer Darren Wilson shot at Michael Brown, an unarmed eighteen-year-old Black man, twelve times, killing him. The tragic incident ignited a powder keg of hostilities and racial tensions between the majority-white Ferguson police force and the Black community it patrolled. The city erupted in violent response to Brown's killing, with protesters shouting, "Hands up, don't shoot," Brown's alleged plea to Officer Wilson before he shot the teen.

There in Ferguson, the Black Lives Matter movement was born.

The origin of the phrase "Black Lives Matter" (BLM) is attributed to the Black novelist, playwright, and essayist James Baldwin. In a 1979 speech at the University of California, Berkeley, Baldwin discussed what he believed were the mounting frustrations of Black people with police brutality and systemic oppression and discrimination, and he reminded America that Black people matter. Black lives matter.

BLM activists, like abolitionists and anti-slavery proponents of past centuries, believe that Black people are entitled to freedom and self-determination without interference or control by white people. Like Frederick Douglass, Harriet Tubman, and other nineteenth-century abolitionists, they believe in organizing, advocating, and speaking truth to power by taking the work to the people.

The BLM Guiding Principles include:

Restorative Justice
Diversity
Empathy
Globalism
Loving Engagement
Being Unapologetically Black
Collective Value
Affirming Black Women
Intergenerational Engagement
Queer and Trans Affirmation

Collectively, these guidelines outline the types of social justice work BLM organizers and advocates are engaged in and how they approach their work.

Their radical strategies reflect the evolution of Black liberation struggles, which are rooted in the abolition and anti-slavery movements of the past.

THE AMERICAN ABOLITION MOVEMENT TODAY

Modern abolition in America is different from the abolition movement to end chattel slavery because many abolitionists today are focused on freeing citizens from the shackles of state and federal prisons. They are working for the abolition of American prisons, or the prison-industrial complex, which houses over 1 million Americans serving sentences in state-run prisons and close to 1 million in federal prisons, tribal jails, local jails, immigrant detention centers, military jails, and other law-enforcement detention facilities.

When the Thirteenth Amendment did away with legal chattel slavery in the United States, it left the door open for other types of slavery—namely, labor camps, local jails, and state and federal prison slavery. The amendment includes a clause that abolishes all slavery "except as a punishment for crime whereof the party shall have been duly convicted." This short passage changed the course of freedom for the newly freed Black population. Yes, they were free, but at any time that could change if they were found guilty of a crime. During Reconstruction, Southern whites weaponized this clause to re-enslave Black men and put them to work for free on work farms and in labor camps.

As Blacks migrated north during the twentieth
century, in search of work and educational opportunities, not only did the populations of cities and towns
change, the number of United States prisons began
to grow as well. American prison populations have
skyrocketed and include people of all races and gen-
ders, and even children in youth detention centers. In
just over fifty years, the number of Americans serving
time in jails and penitentiaries has grown by a whop-
ping 500 percent! In 1970, there were roughly three
hundred thousand incarcerated Americans. Today,
there are over 2 million citizens housed in American
prisons, earning the United States the recognition of
having the largest prison population in the world,
beating out countries with much larger populations.

Black people make up 13 percent of the American population but account for nearly 35 percent of
all prison inmates. Advocates for prison abolition
argue that racism in law enforcement and limited in-
vestment in public schools, affordable housing, jobs
paying livable wages, and healthcare options in poor
communities collectively have led to the astronomi-
cal increase in the Black prisoner population. Unfair
and harsh sentencing for low-level offenses and higher
conviction rates for Black defendants than whites
for the same crimes, often handed down by mostly

or all-white juries, not of their peers, have created a steady pipeline of Black people to prisons nationwide.

These factors often trap poor Black people in dire situations with few options for improving their lives. And, as was the case for the newly emancipated enslaved populations throughout the South, they frequently find themselves in prison for unfairly long stints, often for minor infractions. When this happens, many are forced to work for free, earning money for the prisons that are paid big bucks by companies for the work.

Prison labor is used to make money for state prison systems and big corporations that pay states to use prison labor to manufacture their products and goods. Prison workers are paid just pennies per hour, meaning they don't even earn enough to purchase personal hygiene supplies such as toothpaste. Like chattel slaves and the Black men in the post-slavery work camps and farms, the unpaid prison labor force works long hours without breaks under harsh conditions. Those savings go directly to the big corporations that use their labor for their goods and services.

Prison laborers have no rights, which makes them vulnerable in several ways. Refusal to work can result in physical punishment, negative treatment by guards, unfair rulings by parole boards, and even workplace accidents, from which they have no recourse.

Today there are no plantation owners making money from slavery; instead, private companies and government agencies make huge profits off prison labor. When slavery ended, legal imprisonment for crimes like loitering led to a rising population of incarcerated Black men. They were no longer enslaved by individual white slave owners, but instead free labor for the county and state work farms and prisons that imprisoned them. Over time, prisons, like slavery, became a big business!

Think about this: Each year, the United States spends roughly $80 billion dollars to operate prisons and detention centers nationally. It costs states and municipalities between $23,000 and over $550,000 each year to house, feed, and monitor one prison inmate. Yet states spend between $9,390 and $33,440 per student for education!

Prison abolitionists believe Americans can and should work to collectively devise plans to alleviate the need for prison incarceration by making sure every American has access to housing, food, education, jobs, and healthcare. For example, Abolition Is . . . is an online abolition resource for and by youth who are striving to create a world where "the violences of prisons, policing, and surveillance are obsolete . . . a new world guided by care, collective action, and imagination." According to the Critical Resistance, a prison and policing abolition advocacy organization, "abolition isn't just about getting rid of buildings full of cages. It's also about undoing the society we live in" because the prison industrial complex "both feeds on and maintains oppression and inequalities through punishment" and violence and controls millions of people.

In other words, none of us is free until all of us are free.

RESOURCES FOR YOUNG READERS

BOOKS

Alberti, Enigma, and Tony Cliff. *Mary Bowser and the Civil War Spy Ring.* Workman Publishing, 2019.

Burgan, Michael. *Spies of the Civil War: An Interactive Espionage Adventure.* You Choose: Spies. Capstone Press, 2015.

Cornell, Kari A. *Women in the Civil War.* Essential Library of the Civil War. Essential Library, 2016.

Curtis, Christopher Paul. *Elijah of Buxton.* Scholastic Press, 2007.

Dell, Pamela. *Memoir of Susie King Taylor: A Civil War Nurse.* Capstone Press, 2017.

Doeden, Matt. *Weapons of the Civil War.* Capstone Press, 2008.

Forten, Charlotte. *Diary of Charlotte Forten: A Free Black Girl Before the Civil War.* Capstone Press, 2014.

Hansen, Joyce. *I Thought My Soul Would Rise and Fly: The Diary of Patsy, a Freed Girl.* Dear America. Scholastic, 2011.

Herschbach, Elisabeth. *Black Soldiers in the Civil War.* Focus Readers, 2020.

Jopp, Kelsey. *John Brown and the Harpers Ferry Raid.* Focus Readers, 2020.

Kolpin, Molly. *The Biggest Battles of the Civil War.* Capstone Press, 2014.

Kolpin, Molly. *Great Women of the Civil War.* Capstone Press, 2015.

McKissack, Patricia C. *A Picture of Freedom: The Diary of Clotee, a Slave Girl.* Dear America. Scholastic, 1997.

McMullan, Margaret. *How I Found the Strong.* Clarion Books, 2004.

Micklos Jr., John. *A Primary Source History of the United States Civil War.* Capstone Press, 2016.

Morretta, Alison. *Frederick Douglass and William Garrison: A Partnership for Abolition.* Cavendish Square, 2015.

Murphy, Jim. *The Boys' War: Confederate and Union Soldiers Talk About the Civil War.* Clarion Books, Illustrated Edition, 1993.

Myers, Laurie. *Escape by Night: A Civil War Adventure.* Reprint, Square Fish, 2014.

Owens-Lalude, Judith C. *Miss Lucy: Slave and Civil War Nurse.* Anike Press, 2013.

Reit, Seymour. *Behind Rebel Lines: The Incredible Story of Emma Edmonds, Civil War Spy.* Harcourt Brace, 1988.

Smith, Nikki Shannon. *Ann Fights for Freedom: An Underground Railroad Survival Story.* Girls Survive. Reprint, Stone Arch Books, 2019.

Smith, Nikki Shannon. *Sarah Journeys West: An Oregon Trail Survival Story.* Girls Survive. Stone Arch Books, 2020.

Vonne, Mira. *Gross Facts About the US Civil War.* Gross History. Capstone Press, 2020.

Warren, Andrea. *Under Siege!: Three Children at the Civil War Battle for Vicksburg.* Farrar, Straus and Giroux Books for Young Readers, 2009.

MUSEUMS

1838 Black Metropolis
Philadelphia, Pennsylvania
1838blackmetropolis.com

Banneker-Douglass-Tubman Museum
Annapolis, Maryland
bdmuseum.maryland.gov

The Charleston Museum
Charleston, South Carolina
charlestonmuseum.org

International African American Museum
Charleston, South Carolina
iaamuseum.org/the-museum

The Legacy Museum
Montgomery, Alabama
legacysites.eji.org/about/museum

Lowcountry Digital History Initiative at the College of Charleston
ldhi.library.cofc.edu

Museum of the Reconstruction Era
Columbia, South Carolina
historiccolumbia.org/woodrow-wilson-family-home

National Abolition Hall of Fame and Museum
Peterboro, New York
nationalabolitionhalloffameandmuseum.org

National Civil Rights Museum
Memphis, Tennessee
civilrightsmuseum.org

National Museum of African American History and Culture
Washington, DC
nmaahc.si.edu

Old Slave Mart Museum
Charleston, South Carolina
charleston-sc.gov/160/Old-Slave-Mart-Museum

Whitney Plantation
Wallace, Louisiana
whitneyplantation.org

BIBLIOGRAPHY

"About Abolition Is . . ." Abolition Is . . . abolition-is.com/about.

"An Act to Prohibit the Importation of Slaves . . ." Library of Congress. loc.gov/resource/rbpe.22800200.

"Act to Prohibit the Importation of Slaves 1807." VCU Libraries Social Welfare History Project. socialwelfare.library.vcu.edu/eras/colonial-postrev/act-to-prohibit-the-importation-of-slaves-1807.

Alexander, Kerry Lee. "Frances Ellen Watkins Parker." National Women's History Museum. womenshistory.org/education-resources/biographies/frances-ellen-watkins-harper.

"Anna Murray Douglass." National Park Service. nps.gov/frdo/learn/historyculture/anna-murray-douglass.htm.

"Author, Harriet E. Wilson." The Harriet Wilson Project. harrietwilsonproject.net/wilson-s-novel.html.

"Bass Reeves: The Real Lone Ranger." National Law Enforcement Officers Memorial Fund. nleomf.org/bass-reeves.

"Battle of Gettysburg." history.com/topics/american-civil-war/battle-of-gettysburg.

"Behind the Screen: Unveiling the Real Soldiers of the 54th Massachusetts." *American Battlefield Trust,* February 16, 2024. battlefields.org/learn/articles/head-tilting-history/behind-screen-unveiling-real-soldiers-54th-massachusetts.

"Benjamin O. Davis Sr." National Museum of the United States Army. thenmusa.org/biographies/benjamin-o-davis-sr.

"Benjamin Oliver Davis Sr.: A Biography." US Army Heritage and Education Center. armyheritage.org/wp-content/uploads/2020/06/Benjamin_Oliver_Davis_AHEC_Bio.pdf.

"Black Soldiers in the U.S. Military During the Civil War." National Archives. archives.gov/education/lessons/blacks-civil-war.

Blanc, Cecile. "Where Are the Black Inventors of the Industrial Revolution?" cecileblanc.com/2020/11/08/where-are-the-black-inventors-of-the-industrial-revolution.

"Chancellorsville." American Battlefield Trust. battlefields.org/learn/civil-war/battles/chancellorsville.

"Civil Rights Act of 1875." U.S. Senate. senate.gov/artandhistory/history/common/image/Civil_Rights_Act_1875.htm.

"Civil War Facts: 1861–1865." nps.gov/civilwar/facts.htm.

Clark, Alexis. "When Harriet Tubman Led a Brazen Civil War Raid." history.com/news/harriet-tubman-combahee-ferry-raid-civil-war.

"Constitution Annotated." constitution.congress.gov/browse/essay/artIV-S2-C3-1/ALDE_00013571.

Dalton, Melissa. "A Brief History of the Life of Martin Robison Delany." *Out of the Clock Tower* (blog), February 19, 2021. greenecountyohio.gov/Blog .aspx?IID=294.

Declaration of Independence. National Archives. archives.gov/founding-docs/ declaration-transcript.

"Eliminating Slavery in the World." quakersintheworld.org/quakers-in-action/58.

Erath, John. "Union Success in the Civil War and Lessons for Strategic Leaders." National Defense University Press. ndupress.ndu.edu/Media/News/ Article/581883/union-success-in-the-civil-war-and-lessons-for-strategic-leaders.

Evans, Farrell. "America's First Black Regiment Gained Their Freedom by Fighting Against the British." history.com/news/first-black-regiment-american-revolution -first-rhode-island.

"Exodusters and Western Expansion." National Archives. archives.gov/research/ african-americans/migrations/exodusters.

"First American Abolition Society Founded in Philadelphia." history.com/ this-day-in-history/first-american-abolition-society-founded-in-philadelphia.

"Forced Labor in Prisons." Freedom Network USA. freedomnetworkusa.org/ 2023/08/11/forced-labor-in-prisons.

Fought, Leigh. "On the Life of Black Activist Anna Murray Douglass." Black Perspectives. aaihs.org/on-the-life-of-black-abolitionist-anna-murray-douglass.

Franklin, Benjamin. "An address to the public, from the Pennsylvania Society for promoting the abolition of slavery, and the relief of free negroes, unlawfully held in bondage." Library of Congress. loc.gov/resource/rbpe.14701000/?st=text.

Freeman, Elsie, Wynell Burroughs Schamel, and Jean West. "The Fight for Equal Rights: A Recruiting Poster for Black Soldiers in the Civil War." *Social Education* 56, no. 2 (February 1992): 118–120. Revised and updated in 1999 by Budge Weidman.

Funk, William H. "The Dismal Swamp: One Road Out of Slavery Took You Straight into the Boggiest Place You've Ever Been." *Humanities* 38, no. 2 (Spring 2017).

Gates, Henry Louis, Jr. "The Truth Behind '40 Acres and a Mule.'" The African Americans (PBS). pbs.org/wnet/african-americans-many-rivers-to-cross/history/ the-truth-behind-40-acres-and-a-mule.

"General John A. Logan, Memorial Day Founder."

"Gettysburg." American Battlefield Trust. battlefields.org/learn/civil-war/battles/ gettysburg.

Glaze, Robert L. "Postwar life and the Ku Klux Klan." *Encyclopaedia Brittanica.* britannica.com/biography/Nathan-Bedford-Forrest/Postwar-life-and-the -Ku-Klux-Klan.

"Granville T. Woods." Biography. biography.com/inventors/granville-t-woods.

"Granville T. Woods' Inventions Power Life Still Today." Entergy. entergynewsroom.com/article/granville-t-woods-inventions-power-life-still-today.

"Great Dismal National Wildlife Refuge." U.S. Fish and Wildlife Service.

Greenspan, Jesse. "The Other Targets of John Wilkes Booth's Murder Conspiracy." history.com/news/the-other-targets-of-booths-murder-conspiracy.

Hardingham-Gill, Tamara. "She was the first Black woman to fly in the US Air Force." CNN. May 23, 2024. cnn.com/travel/theresa-claiborne-first-black -woman-air-force-pilot-retirement/index.html.

"Hiram Revels: First African American Senator." *Senate Stories* (blog). United States

States Senate. senate.gov/artandhistory/senate-stories/First-African-American
-Senator.htm.

"Hiram Rhodes Revels." National Park Service. nps.gov/people/hiram-rhodes
-revels.htm

"The Historical Legacy of Watch Night." National Museum of African
American History and Culture, Smithsonian. nmaahc.si.edu/explore/stories/
historical-legacy-watch-night.

"The Journey to Emancipation: The Germantown Protest, 1688."
nmaahc.si.edu/explore/stories/journey-emancipation-germantown-protest-1688.

"Juneteenth." National Museum of African American History and Culture,
Smithsonian. nmaahc.si.edu/juneteenth.

"Juneteenth and the Broken Promise of '40 Acres and a Mule.'" National Farmers
Union. nfu.org/2020/06/19/juneteenth-and-the-broken-promise-of-40-acres
-and-a-mule.

Law, Victoria. "Rethinking Incarceration." Harvard Radcliffe Institute.
radcliffe.harvard.edu/news-and-ideas/rethinking-incarceration.

Lewis, James. "Black Hawk's Intentions in 1832." *Encyclopaedia Brittanica*.
britannica.com/event/Black-Hawk-War/Indian-removal-and-growing-tensions
-in-Illinois.

"Life Story: Susie Baker King Taylor (1848–1912): Black Union Army Worker and
Reconstruction Era Teacher." Women and the American Story. wams.nyhistory
.org/a-nation-divided/reconstruction/susie-baker-king-taylor.

Loving v. Virginia, 388 U.S. 1(1967). supreme.justia.com/cases/federal/us/388/1.

"Major American Political Parties of the 19th Century." Norwich University.
online.norwich.edu/major-american-political-parties-19th-century.

Maranzani, Barbara. "Harriet Tubman: 8 Facts About the Daring Abolitionist."
history.com/news/harriet-tubman-facts-daring-raid.

Markovich, Jeremy. "The Great Dismal Swamp isn't as great, dismal, or swampy
as it used to be." *North Carolina Rabbit Hole*. ncrabbithole.com/p/great-dismal
-swamp-nc-va-not-so-swampy-anymore.

"Martin R. Delany (1812–1885)." Virginia Encyclopedia.
encyclopediavirginia.org/entries/delany-martin-r-1812-1885.

"Membership of the 118th Congress: A Profile." Congressional Research Service.
crsreports.congress.gov/product/pdf/R/R47470.

"Memorial Day: The Origins." General John A. Logan Museum.
loganmuseum.org/memorial-day.

Michales, Debra, ed. "Sojourner Truth:" National Women's History Museum.
womenshistory.org/education-resources/biographies/sojourner-truth.

National Constitution Center Staff. "The forgotten man who almost became
President after Lincoln." *Constitution Daily Blog*. National Constitution Center,
April 2024. constitutioncenter.org/blog/the-forgotten-man-who-almost
-became-president-after-lincoln.

Nellis, Ashley. "Mass Incarceration Trends." The Sentencing Project.
sentencingproject.org/reports/mass-incarceration-trends.

Northup, Solomon. *Twelve Years a Slave: Narrative of Solomon Northup, a Citizen
of New-York, Kidnapped in Washington City in 1841, and Rescued in 1853, from a
Cotton Plantation Near the Red River, in Louisiana*. Documenting the American
South. docsouth.unc.edu/fpn/northup/northup.html.

"Per Pupil Spending by State 2024." *World Population Review.* worldpopulationreview.com/state-rankings/per-pupil-spending-by-state.

Plessy v. Ferguson (1896). National Archives Milestone Documents. archives.gov/milestone-documents/plessy-v-ferguson.

Priggs v. Pennsylvania, 41 U.S. 539 (1842). Justia U.S. Supreme Court. supreme.justia.com/cases/federal/us/41/539.

"Rainey, Joseph Hayne." History, Art & Archives. U.S. House of Representatives. history.house.gov/People/Listing/R/RAINEY,-Joseph-Hayne-(R000016)/.

"Ratifying the Thirteenth Amendment, 1866." The Gilder Lehrman Institute of American History. gilderlehrman.org/history-resources/spotlight-primary-source/ratifying-thirteenth-amendment-1866.

"Reconstruction Timeline." American Experience (PBS). pbs.org/wgbh/americanexperience/features/reconstruction-timeline.

Reeves, Matthew. "Singleton, Benjamin 'Pap.'" civilwaronthewesternborder.org/encyclopedia/singleton-benjamin-%E2%80%9Cpap%E2%80%9D.

Roesch, Hannah. "The Legacy of John A. Logan." *Emerging Civil War.* emergingcivilwar.com/2021/07/13/the-legacy-of-john-a-logan.

Román, Iván. "6 Black Heroes of the Civil War." history.com/news/black-heroes-us-civil-war-tubman-douglass-augusta-smalls-galloway.

Roy, Michaël. *Young Abolitionists: Children of the Antislavery Movement.* New York University Press, 2024. https://nyupress.org/9781479830091/young-abolitionists.

Shane, Scott. *Flee North: A Forgotten Hero and the Fight for Freedom in Slavery's Borderland.* Celadon Books, 2023.

Shane, Scott. "How the Underground Railroad Got Its Name." *New York Times.* September 11, 2023.

"Signals for the Use of the Navy of the Confederate States." Naval History and Heritage Command. history.navy.mil/research/library/online-reading-room/title-list-alphabetically/s/signals-use-navy-confederate-states.html.

"Slavery Timeline." *Digital History.* digitalhistory.uh.edu/era.cfm?eraID=6&smtID=4.

"Sojourner Truth." history.com/topics/black-history/sojourner-truth.

Strode, Hudson. "Capture and Imprisonment of Jefferson Davis." *Encyclopaedia Britannica.* britannica.com/biography/Jefferson-Davis/Capture-and-imprisonment.

USA Facts Team. "How much do states spend on prisoners?" *USA Facts.* usafacts.org/articles/how-much-do-states-spend-on-prisons.

Wallenfeldt, Jeff. "Assassination of Abraham Lincoln." *Encyclopaedia Britannica.* britannica.com/event/assassination-of-Abraham-Lincoln.

"The White House Building." whitehouse.gov/about-the-white-house/the-grounds/the-white-house.

Wilson, Harriet. *Our Nig.* ntu.ac.uk/__data/assets/pdf_file/0023/1126175/Our-Nig.pdf.

Wise, Alana. "Juneteenth Is Now a Federal Holiday." NPR. npr.org/2021/06/17/1007602290/biden-and-harris-will-speak-at-the-bill-signing-making-juneteenth-a-federal-holiday.

IMAGE CREDITS